Meanwhile

Meanwhile

What to Do While You Wait

Amanda Grace
Caldwell

Bold Vision Books
PO Box 2011
Friendswood, Texas 77549

Copyright 2017 @ Amanda Grace Caldwell

Published in the United States of America

ISBN 9780692659465

Cover Art by @ Vladimir Nikulin | Dreamstime.com
Cover Design by kae Creative Solutions

Bold Vision Books
PO Box 2011
Friendswood, Texas 77549
www.boldvisionbooks.com

All rights reserved. No part of this publication may be reproduced, stored in a retrieval system, or transmitted in any form or by any means -- electronic, mechanical, photocopy, recording, or any other -- except for brief quotations in printed reviews, without the prior permission of the publisher.

Unless otherwise marked, Scripture quotations marked are taken from the Holy Bible, NIV®, NIV®. Copyright © 1973, 1978, 1984, 2011 by Biblica, Inc.™ Used by permission of Zondervan. All rights reserved worldwide. www.zondervan.com The "NIV" and "NIV" are trademarks registered in the United States Patent and Trademark Office by Biblica, Inc.™

Scripture quotations marked ESV are taken from The Holy Bible, English Standard Version® (ESV®) Copyright © 2001 by Crossway, a publishing ministry of Good News Publishers. All rights reserved. ESV Text Edition: 2007

Scripture quotations marked THE MESSAGE are taken from THE MESSAGE, copyright© by Eugene H. Person 1993, 1994, 1995, 1996, 2000, 2001, 2002. Used by permission of NavPress Publishing Group.

Certain names, stories and identifying details have been changed to protect the privacy of individuals. This book is not intended as a substitute for the advice of a counselor. The reader should consult a counselor with respect to any symptoms that may require talk therapy or diagnosis.

Dedication

For El Roi, the God who sees and hears us.
All glory and thanks to the One who knows me.

And for my family. You are the greatest gift God
has ever given me.

Table of Contents

Foreword 9

A Note About the Meanwhile 13

Part One-Uprooted
Chapter One: Graduation Day 17
Chapter Two: Perfect Child 22
Chapter Three: Post-College 28
Chapter Four: A New Name 38

Part Two-Pruning
Chapter Five: Disappointment 45
Chapter Six: "Me Too" 59
Chapter Seven: Desire 69
Chapter Eight: Envy 77
Chapter Nine: Indecision 83
Chapter Ten: Grace 88

Part Three-Becoming Rooted
Chapter Eleven: Trust 95
Chapter Twelve: Hope 104
Chapter Thirteen: Waiting Gracefully 109
Chapter Fourteen: Purpose 121
Chapter Fifteen: Giving 132
Chapter Sixteen: Becoming 137
Chapter Seventeen: Decision-Making 144

Part Four-Rooted
Chapter Eighteen: #Adulting 155
Chapter Nineteen: Friendship 162
Chapter Twenty: A $3 Shot of Espresso 170
Chapter Twenty-One: Freedom 176
Chapter Twenty-Two: Graduation Day 180
Chapter Twenty-Three: Suddenly 185

Book List 188

Appendix A 189

Afterword 192

Acknowledgments 195

About the Author 199

Endnotes 200

Foreword

Kelly Taylor

Growing up, I thought life would look a certain way. I planned my future, my husband, our four children and the yellow lab in the front yard. Even when my family faced severe pain and division, I knew everything would work itself out in the end. I wasn't worried.

When we were younger, we knew what was coming next. All of us in fourth grade, auditioning to be the star of the play, awaiting fifth grade. Middle school was filled with awkward dances, volleyball tryouts, and brand-name T-shirts. Notes were passed to friends in the five minutes we had between classes. I dreamt of going to high school where I would finally get my driver's license and tryout for the varsity cheerleading team.

Everyone loved high school, at least everyone in the movies. I knew I would thrive there. I'd go to football games with friends and homecoming dances with boys I didn't care so much about. We studied for our ACT and SAT tests and applied for college. I figured we'd all get into our dream schools. It was all going according to plan.

I knew I wanted to become a wedding planner, so I adjusted my resume as such and interviewed as needed. When things didn't pan out the way I hoped, I didn't sweat it because I had a gut feeling marriage was right around the corner. I pictured our neighborhood and the quaint house my handsome husband purchased for us.

But I'm still waiting. Before the white picket fence, what am I supposed to do with these awkward "in-between" years?

After I graduated college, I began to think, *What am I doing? Why is nothing going according to plan? What's my purpose? How long will I be here? Where am I going?* I found myself disappointed, scared, and filled with emotions I had never before experienced. I was a mess. I didn't know how to move forward and only wanted to go back to those middle school hallways or that college football game. That would at least be familiar.

Looking around, I discovered friends in every stage of life. Some were still in college or wrapping up a master's program, others were married and learning to relate to one's spouse. Some were launching careers or trying to land it big in Los Angeles or New York. I didn't know who I was or what defined me.

By God's grace and in the midst of the confusion, I found Amanda Grace Caldwell. I remember reading her name on a list of seven who formed our new small group. In the quietest of moments, I heard a clear whisper from the Lord: *"I know you don't know her yet, but she will play a big role in your life."* I had chills down my spine and felt the Holy Spirit nudge me to move closer to her. I was curious what God was going to do.

As time unfolded, we began to discuss her upcoming book. She allowed me to read through her manuscript, and while reading it I clung to the chapters and the words. For the first time I read words that accurately expressed how I was feeling. Amanda Grace laid out my all-over-the-map emotions. Her stories and experiences gave me hope in a time of despair. Her words gave me comfort and life in the midst of a confusing and hard chapter. Page after page, I didn't want the story to end.

As I read, I realized something: We need to be comfortable with the *Meanwhile*; comfortable with the discomfort, comfortable with the unknown, and with changes in our plans. This side of eternity we will always be living in some state of tension: the what-was and the what-if, the then and the now, the waiting and the moving on. We will be in the *Meanwhile* until we are Heaven bound. Whether we are waiting for that thing, that desire, that person to change, the overarching ache will remain until God comes again. But, it's a gift from God to work through these tensions at such a young age. And it's a gift from God that He meets us in our day-to-day.

My *Meanwhile* season has been one of becoming, one full of figuring out who I am, who God is, and what He wants for my life and me. It's a season of developing patience and of transformation. I have found meaning and purpose in this stage of life. I needed a guide, a mentor. This book, these questions, and conversations with Amanda Grace have been instrumental in this development. She met a niche for the group of souls who feel like we are drowning in our twenties and thirties.

Meanwhile is not only relatable and honest but it is sprinkled with joy and possibility. Amanda Grace has been a guide, mentor, prayer warrior and cheerleader. Her book has been my lifeline as I have tried my best to navigate these waters. There's a great need for someone to speak love and truth into the hearts of our tribe. Amanda Grace is that woman and *Meanwhile* is that book.

My prayer for you is that you won't fight against the *Meanwhile*, but that you'll receive it as an invitation and breathe it in deeply and absorb it in your bones. I hope you find Christ as the ultimate Guide and Comfort during this season. I pray Amanda Grace speaks to you the way she did to me as it has changed the trajectory of my 20s. I'm glad we're on this journey together!

Kelly Taylor
Friend of Author

A Note about the Meanwhile

My Dear Friend,

I am excited to begin this journey with you. *Meanwhile* is close to my heart and the story is still unfolding. I am a twenty-something navigating the real world, complete with new jobs, new cities, new relationships, and exorbitant rent. I'm guessing you can relate.

My favorite books always make me feel something. Even when I don't remember everything the author said, I always remember what I felt when reading it. I hope you feel less alone when reading this story. And I hope these words bring you comfort.

God sees you and He hears you. He is real and alive. He will equip you to find contentment, to know who you are and where your life is headed. As you use this book as a guide, put yourself in the story. How do these experiences relate to your journey? Listen for what God is teaching and revealing to you.

I am glad you picked up this book. Whether you need comfort, healing, contentment or peace, I pray with you as God meets you along these pages. I hope He does great things for you.

You are loved & seen,
Amanda Grace

PART ONE
UPROOTED

"It's about a girl who is on the cusp of becoming someone. A girl who may not know what she wants right now, and she may not know who she is right now, but who deserves the chance to find out."
~Jodi Picoult - *My Sister's Keeper*

Chapter One
Graduation Day

*Rubber-banded, stretched to snap—it never seems to
stop. The constant change, the ebb and flow, it's hard
to catch a breath. Throw me a rope; give me a chance,
anything to make me float. I plead for a bone and beg
on my knees, 'my God, is this really my twenties?'*

It was Graduation Day. My car was packed. The house was clean and in order, awaiting the next resident. Donning cap, gown, pumps and pearls, I drove myself to the sports arena. The only agenda was shaking a hand and walking across the stage. I had made it! These four years of college had passed in an instant.

Memories flooded my mind as I thought back to dorm rooms carpeted in pink, late nights "studying," and midnight trips for a #6 combo meal. A best friend would marry the weekend after graduation. Meanwhile, I was preparing to move to Colorado to follow my dream of becoming a counselor. I heard the mountains calling my name as I walked across the stage on that Saturday in May.

That day I graduated college, I threw my cap in the air with great hope and pride. Ready for the real world (or so I thought), I looked forward to the next accomplishment. I wasn't planning to totally change the world, but I hoped to at least impact it. I grew up in a generation taught to believe we could do anything. I'm a Millennial. We've received participation ribbons, been overprotected, encouraged, and given much without the matching responsibility for paying it forward. Developmental psychologist Dr. Jeffrey Jensen Arnett, who coined the term "emerging adulthood," is a pioneer in the study of young adults (roughly ages 18-29-year-olds). He calls us emergent adults—no longer teens but not quite adults yet. We're caught in-between.

According to Pew Research Center, Millennials were born between 1981 and 1997 (aged 18-34 as of 2015). Millennials typically live at home with their parents after graduation, get married later, extend their schooling, and keep jobs for a shorter period of time. This in-between period of our lives is fraught with seemingly endless possibilities and opportunities.

With increased freedom, the world at our fingertips, and the endless directions our lives can take, the years between ages 18-30 feel sporadic and scary. Still, we hope. One national survey found that nearly all (96%) of young adults, 18-24 years old, agree that someday they will get to where they want to be in life.

It's the *someday* that plagues us young adults. The midlife crisis has been superseded by the quarter-life crisis. During such a crisis we feel paralyzed by indecision, lost in the meanwhile. We're weighed down with questions such as: What are you going to do now? Where are you working? Are you dating anyone? Where do you want to be in five years? Are you happy?

What do we do when our lives begin to look drastically different from our friends and peers? Growing up, we had similar trajectories and timelines. But post-graduation, change is the only constant. Some of us are single while others are married and having babies. Some have landed high-paying jobs and others are consistently unemployed. Some have roommates and others have purchased their homes.

This in-between phase is not unique to the Millennial generation. However, our particular situation is heightened by several social changes. Christian Smith and Patricia Snell describe these four changes in their book, *Souls in Transition: The Religious & Spiritual Lives of Emerging Adults.*

First, there are a significant number of students pursuing higher education today. With fewer barriers and more opportunities to add years of schooling, the pressure and expectation to do so is huge.

Second, men and women are delaying their commitment to marriage whether due to extended schooling, cohabitation or increased independence. Jeffery Arnett reports in *Emerging Adulthood* the median age for women to marry has increased from 20 in 1950 to 25 in 2000. For men, the average age to marry has increased from 22 to 27 in the same time period.

Third, American parents are more apt to financially support their young adult kids. This choice may stem from duty or fear. According to Robert Schoeni and Karen Ross in "Material Assistance from Families during the Transition to Adulthood," American parents spend roughly $38,340 per child between the ages of 18 and 34 in material assistance. This includes housing, education expenses, food, cash, and more.

The final social change to affect Millennials is the global and economic fluctuations that challenge the stability of a lifelong career. Today, many young adults spend five to ten years "trying on" different jobs before deciding on a long-term career. This delay of commitment to a specific field results in lower financial security over a long period of time and the continued need for additional training and education.

Dr. Arnett uses five specific features to define this "here-not-there" stage of life:

Exploration
Instability
Self-focus
Transition
Possibilities

For women specifically, life in the twenty-first century has changed drastically. Young women in the nineteen-fifties sought to get married and have children. They saw college degrees as the path to land a man. Jobs were temporary time-fillers until the first baby came. Today, however, women match men in many ways. According to the National Center for Education Statistics, fifty-six percent of the undergraduate students in American colleges and universities were women in 2002. According to Bianchi and Spain (1996) and Dey and Hurtado (1999) in *Emerging Adulthood,* women were cited as obtaining as many law and business degrees as men. Emergent adult females lead contrasting lives to our predecessors. With less pressure to marry and begin a family in our early twenties, we, along with our male counterparts, make the most of our freedom.

I'm not sure how to view myself or what group to claim to be a part of. Am I a woman or am I girl? Is it OK to be caught between the two? Am I a full-blown adult or do I still have some growing up to do?

I have mixed emotions about the freedoms and opportunities that come with this "here-not-there" stage of life. Do you? Sometimes I feel expectant and hopeful. Other times, I feel confused and anxious. I feel stuck between contentment and longing.

I assumed life would be easy after graduating college. I thought walking across the stage to receive my college diploma meant I had arrived. I had navigated life easily up to this point. I had achieved the goals I set for myself and I had a close circle of friends. Surely, I could tackle life head-on.

So I left my Texas home to chase my dream of becoming a counselor. I planned to study in the mountains of Colorado. I would hike in the weekend sunshine and spend free time getting to know new friends. I believed the next three years would be like the last 22: easy. Seminary would be like summer camp on steroids, complete with face paint and worship music reverberating through the hallways of school. It would be a literal mountaintop experience. Or, so I thought.

QUESTIONS FOR THE MEANWHILE:

1. What thoughts ran through your mind when you left home for the first time? After you'd been gone for a few years?

2. When you pictured post-college life, what did you anticipate it would look like? How closely does life match those expectations?

3. In what ways is your life similar to and/or different from your friends? Why is this OK? What makes it tricky?

4. What questions do you dread being asked? (For example: Are you seeing anyone? When will you start trying to have kids? What are your finances like?)

Chapter Two
Perfect Child

"As I expected. 'Mary Poppins,
practically perfect in every way."
~Mary Poppins - Mary Poppins, The movie

I was the perfect child, "PC" for short. I remember first grade in Mrs. May's class. Eighteen pairs of little eyes were glued on our teacher, listening intently to her as she read. But I leaned over to tell my friend James a secret.

"Amanda," Mrs. May said, "Are you paying attention?" It was the first time I had ever been called out in class. I zipped my lips and faced her. She continued to read us the story, and although I turned my attention forward like a little toy soldier, James did not. Instead, he decided to tell me a secret. Mrs. May looked at James and me and said, "Both of you are getting moved to yellow! I asked you to be quiet!" I was mortified. The color cards were for good and bad behavior, and yellow was one step closer to red. My face turned red like the card I feared, and the shame burned all the way down the back of my throat. I was silent the rest of the day, trying to decide how to tell my mom that I had gotten in trouble in school.

Later that afternoon, I climbed onto the school bus and took a seat halfway back to hide my embarrassment. When the school bus pulled up to my bus stop, Mom was waiting on the corner. I walked towards the front of the bus, terrified to admit my wrongdoing. Not two seconds later, I started to cry. Mom lovingly asked what was wrong.

Trembling, I told her the story. Then I looked up through my pink-rimmed (and fogged) glasses, waiting for punishment. Instead, my mom smiled. "I'm proud of you," she said, as she gave me a high five. "What, what for?" I stammered. "For having friends, being social and being normal," she said. I let out a small smile. As I brushed away the tears, the shame of the day seemed to wash away.

Despite my mom's encouragement to be a typical child, I still found identity in trying to become the perfect child. I believed people would love me if I behaved impeccably, in the way I defined it. I thought people would consider me pretty if I was thin. I expected people to be my friend if I was poised and nice all the time. Even the goals I set for myself stemmed from my desire to be perfect (or to at least look that way). In high school, that meant wanting to wear the crown of homecoming queen. In college I tied perfection to being an officer in a sorority and having slender arms.

It was Bid Day at Texas A&M University. The week of sorority recruitment had been a blur of parties, hair spray and lip-gloss. Today was the day we would all find out which sorority we'd been invited to join. I was so excited I could hardly stand it!

We boarded buses that took us to the baseball field where we would open our Bid Day invitations. There I was, sitting in a stadium seat among the hundreds of girls all waiting for their letters. We sat with our rotation groups as our leader passed out each letter. I thumped the envelope against my knee as I waited to be told to open it.

"On the count of three, open up your letters," the announcer said, "ONE, TWO, THREE!" I heard squeals as girls ripped open their envelopes. I tore my letter open and screamed, "Kappa Alpha Theta!" I looked behind my row of seats to my roommate Mandy. "What did you get?" "Theta!" We had each both gotten our number one choice; we would be sorority sisters!

I ran up the few steps to Mandy. We hugged. Then we began to look for our friend, Brittany. She caught our attention. "I got Theta!" We were going to be in the same sorority!

Mandy, Brittany, and I took a quick picture before taking the short ride to sorority row to meet our pledge class and the older Theta members.

The bus turned right onto Athens Drive, and I heard singing coming from all of the different Greek houses as we made our way to the end of the street. There it was. The pale blue and white trimmed Theta house, complete with wraparound porch and porch swings. *I'm home*, I thought as we stepped off the bus. Girls screamed and hugged all around me. Cameras flashed as girls reunited with family members who had come into town to celebrate, and we were presented with armfuls of gifts.

My eye was drawn to the president of our sorority. She was tall and beautiful with short blonde hair. The evening before on preference night, she gave a speech recalling how much Theta meant to her and how she hoped we would feel the same. She looked so majestic up on the stage in her fitted black dress and sleek blonde hair. As I snapped back to reality and was ushered inside of the front door, I thought to myself, *I want to be like her one day. I want to be the president.*

Two and a half years later, it was preference night once again. I stepped into a short, black dress and slipped my pink painted toenails into a pair of black pumps. I snapped on my pearls and looked in the mirror as I fastened my president's pin to my dress. It was a dream come true.

I sought perfection in accomplishment. A 3.0 wasn't good enough as a grade point average. Running a few miles didn't cut it. I wanted to run a half-marathon. Being liked wasn't enough either. I wanted to be everybody's friend. So much so, I filled my calendar to the brim with coffee dates and lunch dates.

I weighed perfection on the scale. I connected skinniness with good things happening. I became the homecoming queen after losing weight in high school, and I became the president of my sorority after running a half marathon and getting in shape. Even though a crown and losing weight never satisfied, I still sought love through the way I looked and in the way I acted such as listening well, being kind and having an open-door policy for sorority members when I was president.

I kept a record of everything I ate and tracked every calorie. The tracking was time-consuming, but I wanted people to like me and I thought being thin was the trick. I used my weight and body image as a means of controlling situations. This method was exhausting but I didn't yet know how heavy the consequences would become.

I worked at being the perfect person like it was my job. I mistakenly believed God wanted me to be perfect too. I thought I had to be the good girl to win His affection. When good things happened growing up, I believed that God had given them to me because I was good, because I had behaved perfectly. The Santa-god I created in my head gave good gifts to the kids on the nice list, and something worse to the kids on the naughty list—or so I thought.

While in college, there was only one thing unchecked on my to-do list of accomplishment—an engagement ring. The Southern expectation was to be engaged at an early age. I grew up dreaming of getting married. Even so, I had other dreams I wanted to accomplish first and commitment terrified me. Was I ready to give up my freedom? What if I chose wrong? Would pursuing one dream take away the cance for the other? Despite the fear, I still longed for the companionship and intimacy marriage brings.

I went to a university where the mantra was "Ring before Spring." It's typical for a girl to get engaged during her senior year of college. There's even a tree called The Century Tree in the middle of campus dedicated to engagements. Legend says that if you walk beneath The Century Tree with your boyfriend or girlfriend, the two of you will marry.

Marriage is good and holy. I simply hadn't learned the healthy balance of commitment with independence.

This theme of dichotomy has followed me into my late twenties. I don't always know how to hold my desires. Sometimes, they go together. Other times, they seem in opposition to one another. I want adventure, and I want to be settled. I want freedom, but I want to be anchored. I want companionship, but fear losing my independence. My twenties have been filled with dichotomies. I've had to find my way through the confusion.

The college sorority house added to the tension I felt. I lived on the second floor of the house and had to cross through the dining room to get to the kitchen. One afternoon I walked by a group of girls flipping through bridal magazines and talking about the dresses they liked and what kind of veils they wanted.

As I twisted off the cap from my peanut butter in the kitchen, I heard the girls giggle. I spread the peanut butter onto my apple and put the jar back in the refrigerator. Walking back through the dining room, I told myself, *"It's okay, you have a plan for your future too."* Getting engaged at 22 was what was expected of me. A large part of me longed for it. But, even though I had other goals I wanted to accomplish first, my naked ring finger made me feel insecure. If there wasn't going to be a ring by spring, I hoped life after college would be as dreamy as those picture-perfect magazine weddings.

Special Note to Readers:

Outside of God's love, the ache we experience in life will never go away. Talk to a Christian counselor if you find yourself purging, restricting, binging or over-exercising. You are loved and you are good enough. The ideal weight or the extra meal will only make you feel emptier.

QUESTIONS FOR THE MEANWHILE:

1. At what point(s) in your life did you realize things were turning out differently than expected? Were these differences due to your expectations or those of others? What was good about the differences you experienced? What was tough about these differences?

2. How did family or friends help you to be yourself, to honor God, and to find your way?

3. What un-truths did you choose to believe—such as one path in life is better than another? Or one dream would take away your chance to accomplish others? What truths have now taken the place of those lies? What boxes on your list have remained unchecked over the years? What boxes have been checked?

4. How do you relate to the desire to be perfect and good? If you don't feel pressured by these, what do you feel pressured by? What pressures are helpful and what pressures are harmful?

5. Based on the dichotomies you have experienced in your life, what are God's next steps to helping you understand your desires and finding peace?

Chapter Three
Post-College

"We never know what God has up His sleeve.
You never know what might happen."
~Elisabeth Elliot

There's something depressing about a dimly lit diner. That was my first thought as my dad and I crossed the state line into Colorado and pulled over for breakfast. My Rocky Mountain Reality was beginning to settle in. We had pulled a trailer for 15 hours before arriving in Denver, my home for the next three years. I felt both elated and terrified from the start. I knew I was on the cusp of something beautiful, but my fantasy was about to crack—like the egg in the frying pan.

After Dad and I entered my new apartment we walked upstairs and onto the balcony. I looked out at the most breathtaking view I had ever seen. A line of Aspen trees bordered the trail behind my apartment and in the distance were those big, purple mountains I had heard calling my name. I hadn't realized they actually looked purple in real life. I thought those were merely words from a song.

Dad and I unwrapped trinket after treasure in my white-walled apartment. With every nail I drove through the wall, I anticipated my grand adventure with a low-level of anxiety:

- Climb a mountain.
- Meet a friend or two.
- Finish seminary early.

- Become the perfect counselor.
- Get baptized after graduation.
- Get married.

The plan felt easy and attainable. But life seldom goes according to plan. I just didn't know that yet. But, it's ok. God can and will still make it good.

New to Town

Sherri was my first friend in Colorado. Sherri worked in an antique store, located on the charming downtown square of Denver suburb Littleton, CO. A short white picket fence stood curbside around the small house overflowing with beautiful finds.

When I entered the treasure trove, I fell in love. Books bound in red and blue lined the shelves. Lace draped the furniture. Old-timey windows graced the walls. I delighted in the array of wonders, floral scents, and delicate comforts.

I happened upon Sherri's shop because I had hauled two antique windows all the way from my family's farm in Brenham, Texas. Though they had made the trip without the slightest crack or splinter (Thanks to Dad's patience and the constant reminder to drive with caution) my windows were 100 years old and needed some TLC before being displayed.

Sherri refinished them for me. As I commented on how lovely I thought the windows looked and paid her for her work, we started a new friendship.

Being new to town works like that sometimes. You find friends in the strangest of places and in the strangest of ways. I felt less anxious knowing that Sherri knew my name. I had her phone number in case something went wrong. She was the first of God's many provisions. He brought Sherri, a kind woman who said I could call her if I ever needed anything.

I missed out on a lot when I first moved to Denver. Looking back, I wish I had made a bucket list from the start: a list of all the things I wanted to experience and all the places I wanted to visit while living in

Colorado. I eventually made such a list. Here are a few things I wrote down:

1. ~~See a concert at Red Rocks Amphitheatre~~

2. ~~Visit the Broadmoor Hotel and dance at the piano bar~~

3. Hike the Incline @ The Garden of Gods

4. ~~Visit Vail~~

5. ~~Explore Aspen with friends~~

6. Take a picture at the (colorful) Colorado sign

7. ~~Go to a Farmers Market on South Pearl Street~~

8. Climb Pikes Peak in Colorado Springs

9. Go white water rafting

10. Go camping with friends

11. ~~Run the BolderBoulder in Boulder~~

12. ~~Eat at the Flagstaff restaurant in Boulder~~

13. ~~Go horseback riding through the mountains~~

14. ~~Go to Jazz in the Park in Downtown Denver~~

If you are new to town, make a bucket list to help you explore your new city. Include new experiences as well as those that are familiar. Invite a friend to join you. This way, you get to go on an adventure and connect with someone new.

Loneliness

Being new to town can bring loneliness. It's expected, but it still surprises. I grew up with some of the best friends a girl could ask for. Really. I think you'd love them too if you got to meet them. It was a bittersweet goodbye. The bitterness came when I realized our lives were beginning to look different from one another. The sweetness remained because these friends continued to know me and love me deeply. The only problem was they were 1,028 miles away.

Annemarie is one of those friends. She's a head taller, a year younger, and about ten years wiser. I met Annemarie the summer before my senior year of college. We had each enrolled in a supply chain management course. We bonded instantly. I call her a soul friend. Soul friends are the ones you feel safe enough with to exhale when you sit across from them at the table. Throughout my senior year, Annemarie and I sat at such a table weekly. We met on Thursday afternoons for chai tea lattes, muffins, and good-for-your-soul conversations. We prayed together, studied the Bible, talked, and did the day-to-day together.

I now realize how rich of a luxury it is to share the details of your life with someone in friendship. It took a move to the mountains where I didn't yet have a soul friend nearby to appreciate that. There I recognized how precious friendship is and how impossible it is to live without connection.

I have never known loneliness like the kind I experienced in Denver. My first friend was Sherri, but loneliness was my closest companion. Living in the hush of the mountains, everything else grew louder. Loneliness became the noise I couldn't quiet when I tried to sleep. Loneliness became the feeling I felt in a crowded room. Loneliness became my reality.

Annemarie had moved to College Station from New Jersey to attend Texas A&M University. I knew she would understand what it felt like to be new to town and to be lonely. So I asked her for advice. She said, "I think most girls graduate with this picture perfect view of the post-college, big-girl world. We think we're ready to ride our bikes at full-speed. But as we begin to navigate the transitions after college, we find bumps and potholes along the way. For the first time in our lives, we no longer know the plan and we feel alone."

I eventually learned how to handle loneliness. On days I felt alone, I'd walk back to that antique store in Littleton. I'd look at the treasures hanging on the walls and marvel in the beauty of simple things. I'd walk down the sidewalk and get a coffee and bar of chocolate at the local chocolate store. Quite simply, I put myself in the proximity of people and places I enjoyed. I felt less alone when I saw people holding hands or heard the espresso machine roar. Being around people in public places helped. What didn't help was spending days at home with my slippers on, flipping through pictures of my friends or toying with social media.

Loneliness is a given when moving to a new place. What we choose to do with the feeling (and where we choose to feel it) makes all the difference.

Routine takes time, it always does. It will take trial by error to find your grocery store, bank and dry cleaners. It will take longer to discover the best neighborhood restaurants and all the short cuts through traffic. If we make a goal to change slowly, instead of quickly, we'll end up showing ourselves more grace and less frustration. Let's remember: haste makes waste.

I like to call the twenties my "tent years." Sometimes, I have a hard time with the transience of the season. There are areas of my life unsettled but that's okay. It helps to focus on the stability of God instead of the instability of the season. God *was* good yesterday, He *will be* good tomorrow and He *is* good right now.

Millennials live in a more technologically connected world than ever before. According to SDL, a leader in language translation and global content management, Millennials in the United States touch their smart phones 45 times a day. The Pew Research Center cites that 87 percent of Millennials use Facebook, 53 percent use Instagram, 37 percent use Twitter and 34 percent use Pinterest.

The statistics are staggering. We Millennials pin and post our way to perceived significance. Social media feeds our discontentment because we always lose in the comparison. We will wrongly elevate ourselves or wrongly diminish ourselves. We compare all that we know about ourselves (the good, bad and ugly) with the seemingly perfect we see.

My sister Lindsey once said we have the power to make people believe anything we want them to on social media. We are the generation that coined the phrase "FOMO," the fear of missing out. We constantly wonder, is there something better happening elsewhere? Social media only exacerbates this fear.

"Facebook Depression" is a new phenomenon according to the American Academy of Pediatrics. It is reported that extended amounts of time on social media sites, such as Facebook, can trigger classic symptoms of depression. These include self-loathing, feelings of hopelessness, and anger. I can relate. I used social media to comfort myself on lonely nights in Denver. I bought into the lie that I would feel more connected to people by liking their pictures or commenting on their posts. But, I only became more isolated and lonely.

Christmas Morning

As a kid, I never slept the night before the first day of school. I would lie awake, too excited for the chance to sharpen my new pencils and wear my first-day-of-school outfit. My first day of seminary felt like Christmas morning. I could hardly wait. I had dreamt of becoming a counselor since I was 13. I tried on a few shirt options and finally settled on one with a longhorn steer on the front. The shirt felt like Texas to me. I packed my red leather tote for my first class.

Counseling Foundations was my first class that morning. We would learn the basics of becoming a counselor in that class. I walked into the classroom, brimming with excitement, and chose a seat front row center. I surveyed the faces in the room. *Who would my friends be? What would class be like?* Following the introductions, I answered three of the professor's questions. The girl next to me noticed my eagerness, "Are you always like this?"

I blinked back my embarrassment. I felt self-conscious by my neighbor's comment initially. But it got my attention. Perhaps, I needed to calm down and settle in.

The Clinic

The first-day excitement propelled me through the next few weeks. Then I entered a counseling room.

Halfway through the semester, our Counseling Foundations class split into two groups for the purpose of practicing our newfound counseling skills on one another.

The assignment seemed simple. One person would be the counselor, another would be the client, and the third would observe. Each of our sessions was recorded so we could transcribe it afterward and turn it in to our professor. I went through the list of skills we had been learning: how to reframe, how to summarize, and how to reflect. I thought about the questions we were supposed to ask. *How does that make you feel? What do you think is beneath that fear?*

I enjoyed the control of the counselor's seat, but I hadn't considered the vulnerability of the client's couch.

I was first to be the client in my group. As I sat on the couch, my mind began to race. *What are they thinking as they look at me? Do they notice my twitching?*

When my classmate-turned-counselor began asking questions, first about my family and then about my friendships back home, I felt scared to share. I talked about my homesickness and my relationship with my boyfriend. I felt naked, with no place to hide. "How did being the perfect child affect you growing up?" *Does she notice I'm wringing my hands? Even that stupid recorder is going to know everything.*

Looking back, that first counseling exercise was scary but it was helpful. I was given a chance to process my emotions and empathize with what my clients would eventually feel sitting on that couch. It is scary to share our hearts and stories with a stranger. But, when met with acceptance, any amount of shame and pain can wash away.

A first counseling session always involves an intake and a disclosure statement. While every form is worded differently, all forms explain that the counseling process can have a disorienting effect on someone. The process felt foreign to me. Eventually, the unraveling would save me. But at the time, it felt messy. For the first time in my life, I could no longer hide my imperfections. By the end of my first semester of classes, I was a teary twenty-three-year old teeming with insecurity. Life after college wasn't living up to my dream. I was lonely, homesick and unsure about my career.

QUESTIONS FOR THE MEANWHILE:

1. How have your moves affected you over the years? In what cities have you lived? What jobs have you taken or what schooling did you begin?

2. What have you learned from your experiences of loneliness? What has helped you in the past to curb the feeling?

3. Do you think you have had, or will have, a quarter-life crisis? Why or why not? What kind of new realities have led, or could lead you, to a quarter-life crisis?

4. Name several instances of comparing yourself to others. How does your view of self match what God says about you?

5. What method do you use for comparison? (e.g. looks, lifestyle, etc.)

6. What kind of affirmation do you seek when you post on social media? *Here's my challenge for all of us:* Let's refrain if it's for selfish gain or from a place of discontentment.

7. If you were to give up social media for 40 days, what impact would that have on your life?

8. Change takes patience and gentleness. What is one way you can slow your pace? What's one way you can be patient with yourself today?

Counselor's Corner

Make a list of "I Am" Statements

We will always be the losing party in the game of comparison. Instead, we need to remember who we are and "Whose" we are. In the table below, write a list of "I Am" statements that are true about you. Include what God says about you. Read these statements to yourself when you feel discontent and defeated. I have included a few of my "I Am" statements to help you begin:

I am wise.	I am kind.	I am brave.	I can do hard things.
I am loved.	I am known.	I am enough.	I am redeemed.
I am heard.	I am seen.	I am not forgotten.	I am secure in God.

Scripture to Memorize

"According to your love remember me, for you are good ... Turn to me and be gracious to me, for I am lonely and afflicted. The troubles of my heart have multiplied; free me from my anguish." (Psalm 25: 7; 16-17 NIV).

*Appendix A includes Bible verses I clung to while in Denver. Each verse is associated with a feeling. Memorize, recite and meditate on these Scriptures. They will help you recognize Truth that leads to feeling less alone. Create your list of Scriptures to build your life upon.

Chapter Four
A New Name

*"Rather than admitting you don't know
what to do next, you fake it in public and
feel lost when you're alone."*
~Emily Freeman - Grace for the Good Girl

The final assignment of my first semester in seminary was a 30-page paper for my Human Development and Counseling Theories class. The goal of the paper was to address my personal development over the years and to integrate that development with theological principles. In order to write about my development, I had to assess my progression through developmental psychologist Erik Erikson's eight social developmental stages. According to Erikson, adolescents navigate through the stage of identity versus role confusion. If an adolescent successfully navigates this stage, he or she will find a solid identity. But if he or she is unable to navigate this stage in a healthy way, he or she will end up in role confusion.

One of the five hallmarks of emerging adulthood is Identity Exploration, as Jeffery Arnett has described. I thought I knew who I was when I moved away to attend seminary. I was a confident college graduate, and I had a picture in my head of what my life would look like after graduation. Through his research, Arnett has extended this adolescence stage into the young adult years. Erikson originally described these young adult years as the Intimacy vs. Isolation stage. However, with the delay of marriage and the postponement of identity development, young adults can find themselves stuck in the Identity vs. Role Confusion stage.

This extension of the Identity Exploration stage became clear in my paper. Throughout the paper, I had to counsel myself through a current issue in my life alongside my success and failure in the navigation of these developmental stages. I chose my identity as the perfect child and how I thought I had to be good enough to be liked by others and loved by God.

One afternoon I sat in the student center working on the paper. My friend Elizabeth from my Counseling Foundations small group sat next to me. Winter had settled in, so I was dressed in a puffy vest and socks up to my knees. I smelled black coffee being poured at the coffee bar, and I looked ahead at the crackling fire, stuck.

What Biblical concept refutes perfectionism? I thought. I had no idea, but I was supposed to disprove it with something. I tapped my fingers against the computer keys and turned up my music. Perhaps Taylor Swift could help me focus. *It's not that hard, Amanda Grace. Just think. What is the opposite of perfectionism?* I leaned my vest against the wooden chair and tried to brainstorm. *Is it mercy? No, I don't think that's right. Love? Maybe so, but that still doesn't sound right.* A few minutes later I gave up and leaned toward Elizabeth. "What did God give us so that we don't need to be perfect?" I asked.

Elizabeth stopped typing as a smile stretched across her face. "Grace, Amanda Grace. Don't you know your middle name?" She laughed. I let out a chuckle and said, "Oh, right. I knew that." But, I didn't. My eyes widened at the reality. I changed my name when I moved to Denver. I grew up being called "Amanda," but there were three Amanda's in my first grade class alone. I didn't know anyone in Colorado so moving to the mountains was my chance for a fresh slate and a new identity by adding my middle name: Amanda Grace. At the time, I didn't understand the significance of my name. I thought I had to be perfect to be favored but God said grace is always free. And it is God's grace that saved me.

Elizabeth had brought to surface something I'd missed while growing up in the church. *What did grace mean anyway?* I looked up the definition and read what it said. "Unmerited favor." I didn't yet comprehend what that meant, but it sure sounded nice.

We Millennials are a confident bunch. We grew up in a culture of self-improvement, self-importance, and self-absorption. We look toward our futures with the utmost optimism. But we also seek others' approval. I sought perfection so that I could control what others thought of me. I hadn't thought to make room in the U-Haul for God's grace. I had forgotten to pack a lot of the right things: grace, hope and trust.

Elizabeth, the one who revealed grace to me, became a dear friend. She had moved to Denver from Virginia, and after a year of scooping coffee beans while living at home with her parents, she had faced her new reality after college. When I realized that the identity I had built was indeed faulty, I asked Elizabeth how she had done it. "How did you find your identity in the *Meanwhile*?"

Elizabeth explained, "I came to realize that superheroes wear stupid costumes, the exchange rate is depressing, and the job market isn't what it used to be anyways. But we ought to let that go. We want to finish first, to make it to this final destination so that we can say that we have arrived. But success can't be who we are. We all have different definitions of success. For some, it's the dream job or starting a family. For others, it might be becoming a world traveler or ending world hunger. But my identity can't be founded on finding success. Try as I might, the fulfillment of my deepest longings were never found in the things I sought so hard after. To be honest, I haven't fully found that satisfaction, but I think that's okay. We were never meant to find total fulfillment on this side of Heaven. Every once in a while I have to take that longing, give her a good pat on the back, and remind her that fulfillment is not her job."

Elizabeth helped me to see that I faced disappointment in Denver because I sought fulfillment in the dream. I had expected the transition from sea level to mile-high elevation to be easy. But, I was coming to realize there was a better way to live than chasing perfection.

QUESTIONS FOR THE MEANWHILE:

1. How would you describe or explain grace to a child? What have you learned about grace recently?

2. How has grace impacted the way you view yourself? The way you view other people? The way you view God?

3. Describe your identity exploration. How has the process looked and felt? What types of identities have you tried on? Which of these have failed? Which have you kept?

PART TWO
PRUNING

"Give me all of you! I don't want so much of your time, so much of your talents and money, and so much of your work. I want you! All of you! I have not come to torment or frustrate the natural man or woman, but to kill it! No half measures will do. I don't want to only prune a branch here and a branch there; rather I want the whole tree out! Hand it over to me, the whole outfit, all of your desires, all of your wants and wishes and dreams. Turn them ALL over to me, give yourself to me and I will make of you a new self—in my image. Give me yourself and in exchange I will give you Myself. My will, shall become your will. My heart, shall become your heart."

~C.S. Lewis - *Mere Christianity*

Chapter Five
Disappointment

"Broken hearts don't heal on anyone's timelines."
~Ann Voskamp

I once met a boy who changed everything. His name was John. The first time I met him, he was awkwardly leaning against the doorframe of my freshman year dorm room. I didn't know it then but he would influence my life more than anyone else had up to that point.

It was springtime in Texas and halfway through junior year. The grass was green, the sun was bright, and the birds were singing their melodies in the high trees. I decided to attend an off-campus luncheon at the home of a couple who were longtime supporters of Texas A&M University. As I entered the house, someone caught my eye. It was John. He stood next to a rock column near the living room, and I walked toward him. "I'm not sure if you remember me, but I'm Amanda. I met you freshman year."

"Of course I remember you!" he smiled. "It's good to see you."

I didn't talk to anyone else as charming as he was during that luncheon, and as I walked back to my car later that afternoon, I felt something I hadn't in a long time: excitement. John had an inviting sparkle in his brown eyes, and I was intrigued.

A few days later, I saw him on campus. A smile broke out across my face as he asked how I was doing. "I'm doing well. I'm headed home to work on a group project for our marketing sales class." As we talked, I felt the same curiosity and excitement as before. I liked that

John was more interested in finding out about me than talking about himself.

He asked for my phone number. "I'm headed out of town for Easter, but when I get back, let's catch up. We could get breakfast one morning?"

"That would be great!" I said. A week passed, and John called. We made plans to eat breakfast tacos at a favorite Bar-B-Q spot in town.

On Saturday morning, I ran down the stairs and out the back door, eager to see how this date would turn out. I slid into John's car, and we made the short trip to Rudy's, one street up from sorority row. We ordered egg and bacon tacos on flour tortillas and two cups of coffee. John prayed over our breakfast and our time together as he held my hand and thanked the Lord for his new friend. I felt my heart thump again. I opened my eyes and smiled at the man across from me. *There's something different about him. I can see it in his eyes.*

"What made you want to be a counselor?" John asked. "And what about Jesus?" "How did you two meet?" Each question brought with it an invitation to share my heart with him. John never added commentary. He listened. I had never felt heard like that before. At the end of breakfast, my heart was full of hope. Maybe this was the man I had been waiting for?

John and I continued to spend time together as friends over the next couple of months. College Station felt like a ghost town that summer with so many students gone from our small college town.

My relationship with food and control had turned sour once again as I helped plan for sorority recruitment in August, so I decided to go home to recoup before the semester began. My disordered eating had begun while dieting in high school but in college, I became addicted to running. I ran for miles every day but barely ate enough afterwards, which left me shaking at football games on Saturday afternoons. I was never present with the people I loved at meals because I was too consumed with myself. I was distracted by the calories I was eating; how tight my pants were fitting and the fear I was getting larger. While carrying on a conversation, lies ran through my head: *I'm not good enough. I'm not pretty enough. I'm not thin enough.* The more weight I lost, the unhappier I became. It was exhausting.

I was stuck on a never-ending pendulum: overeat one day and restrict the next. I recall eating 7 cupcakes at a party in college. I ate each in a different spot so no one would be able to trace the wrappers back to me. Here's the thing about disorderly living (and eating): we're all just trying to fill our God-shaped holes. In my desire for approval, I had become insatiable.

I was upstairs folding my shirts and packing my suitcase when I heard a knock on the door.

I'm not expecting anyone. Then I saw John in the window. *What is he doing here?* John had asked me to be his girlfriend the week before but I had told him no. I expected to find a man like my dad, who played football. John played the trumpet. I figured I'd be with a man who led with dominance. John was kind. I assumed I'd have to fight for affection but John loved. He loved deeply and widely, and it didn't only reach to me, it touched everyone around him.

And even though I had said no, he was there on my front steps.

I let him in. "Hey John, what's going on? Is everything okay?"

"I knew you were headed home today, and I am worried about you, so I wanted to check on you. Please take care of yourself." I had shared the reason for my departure with him—my disordered eating—and was comforted by the warmth and concern with which he spoke.

I blinked back my disbelief and relaxed my tensed shoulders. "Oh, well, thank you. I really appreciate that." We talked for a while longer before he left. As I closed the front door behind him, I wondered, *who is this man and why does he care so much about me?*

After six weeks at home I returned to College Station, whole and content. John and I met for iced coffees at the local coffee shop. As I sat across from him at the tiny two-top table, I felt a nudge toward him deep down in my spirit. My heart began to melt as we talked about my final year of college. That afternoon I decided I wanted to date this man. He was nothing I expected but he was everything I needed. John was someone who made me more of the person God created me to be.

I realized what made John so different. He was more like Jesus than anyone I had ever met. His love for me was healing because it was sacrificial and deep and unconditional. His acceptance of me was a balm to my insecurity. At the time, John was one of the only people I could eat a meal with and not be consumed with calorie counting. One night in particular, we went to see *Beauty and the Beast* at the local theatre. After the show, we picked up a funnel cake and two sodas to share. As we sat there, fighting over pieces of fried dough, I tilted my head back and started to laugh. I felt free and safe in the arms and presence of John.

John and I loved to take long road trips. We'd pack a bag of healthy snacks and load up on Starbucks or Sonic drinks for the drive. We took turns being in charge of music, and it was my turn. I assumed my usual spot as I climbed into the passenger's seat and put my feet up on the dashboard. As we pulled out of the driveway and headed out of College Station, I began to fumble through my iPod to see what song I wanted to play. After scrolling for a few minutes, I landed on our favorite hymn—"It is Well"—because it was.

I leaned my head back against the seat as the music began to play. I looked over at John before glancing out the window. "You always do that," he said, smiling.

"Do what?" I asked, wondering what he meant.

"You always pick a song based on what you're feeling, no matter what that feeling may be."

Tears filled my eyes. No one had ever noticed before. I smiled and looked back out the window, peaceful and content. Finding John was like coming home. I felt so known. Neither of us spoke for fear we'd ruin the moment. He knew the layers of my heart because God had given him the eyes to see them—to see me.

When I chose to move to Colorado to go to seminary, John and I decided to date from afar. The plan was for him to join me in the mountains after he finished his undergraduate degree a year later. When I felt homesick and overwhelmed, I clung to him to make me feel better. At times, I depended on him too much. I expected John to help take the anxiety away. But, despite his constant care, something didn't feel right.

The initial doubt I experienced when John asked me to be his girlfriend surfaced again after moving to Colorado. *How could this be?* I thought. *He's the best man I have ever known. He has to be the one.*

I couldn't shake the doubt I had about moving forward in dating John. A break-up was not in the plan and losing him terrified me. But the more we talked on the phone and the more I flew back and forth between Colorado and Texas, the uneasier I became. In an effort to make the anxiety go away, I decided to make a plan.

I marched into my advisor's office two months after school began. I handed Mrs. Sharon my degree plan, rumpled in my clinched hand, and explained to her that I needed to finish school quick. I told her my boyfriend and I were talking about getting married, and I wanted to be done in two years. I thought I could keep the anxiety at bay if I took control of the situation.

Mrs. Sharon kindly listened to my frantic voice and said, "Pushing yourself to finish in two years is not something I'd necessarily suggest, but yes, it is possible. Just be sure you don't speed too quickly through this process and end up missing out on the lessons along the way." I walked out of the office determined to graduate early. Surely, I could find contentment the quicker seminary would end.

I wanted to be married. I was so confused. Here was this incredible man in front of me. *Why wasn't I choosing him? Why would God bring me such a good man if we wouldn't end up together in the end?*

Classes were officially over for the semester and I turned in my 30-page paper about grace and perfectionism. I decided to celebrate the end of our first semester by inviting Elizabeth over to watch a movie. It was a Friday night and earlier that day, I had signed up for 15 credit hours (9 credit hours is considered full-time) for the spring semester in order to graduate early. I didn't want seminary to last longer than it needed to. It wasn't living up to what I had imagined. I had kept my uneasiness about John to myself but as the movie credits rolled across the screen, my angst spilled over. With tears, I said, "I think I need to break up with him."

Dr. Jeffery Arnett says that the Millennial generation sets itself up for unhappiness and disappointment because we grew up with so much and we expect so much. I broke up with John two days after I landed back in Texas for Christmas break. I was destroyed. The pain cut deep like a knife punctures the skin. I grieved the loss of the picture I had painted for my life and future almost as much as I grieved losing John.

I turned my back on God. If He were good, I wouldn't feel so confused. Losing John was the final straw. I was homesick and lost before. Now, I felt utterly alone. I blamed God even though He had nothing to do with it.

Circumstances had taught me I could accomplish whatever I want and be whomever I want. I never bargained for disappointment so I was derailed by unmet expectation. I didn't realize it then but we won't get everything we want in life. I grew up entitled to a pain-free life.

When I broke up with John, it was like leaving home all over again. "This isn't what you called me to," I told God. "How am I supposed to do this alone?"

That Christmas lacked the usual tinsel and joy.

I thought I was being obedient by breaking up with John. I assumed that if I broke up with him, the anxiety would go away. But it didn't. Things only got worse. Why would the Santa-god I had grown up believing in do this to me? I was confused.

At the end of Christmas break, I flew back to Colorado for an intersession class at school before the spring semester officially began. For a week, we met six hours a day. The only thing more harrowing than the length of the class was the freezing temperature outside. Every morning, I'd try to keep the wind from hitting my face as I walked to the classroom from the parking lot. *Cold like my soul. Bitter like my heart.*

One morning, I was crunching through the snow when I saw a goose waddle across my path. I had never seen a lone goose before. They usually traveled in gaggles. He began to cry a low, mournful song. *Me too, Mr. Goose, me too.* Later that week, I sat down to write in my journal:

Dear Lord,

So this is the breaking point. If I don't have John to take care of me, I have to believe you can and you will. There's not a plan in mind or a friend beside. I am lonely and scared and confused. I don't even know how to trust you again. I am messy and unsure. I need your grace to restore all that hurts. The misses, hurts, and bruises. I want a buddy, a lover, a friend. I'm terrified to sit alone with my thoughts, my sadness, and my indecision.

I want to fix, to mend, but I'm terrified to begin feeling the anger, loneliness, hurt, sadness and depression. God, make this pain go away. And if you won't take it away, please plunge into it with me. If this is rock bottom, I have to believe that I'm still breathing and right below the floor is your hand. Will you please meet me in all this mess? You're all I have left.

Christian Smith and Patricia Snell explain in their work, *Souls in Transition,* that the years between adolescence and emergent adulthood cause some Millennials to feel far from God or to lose belief in Him altogether. I was one of those Millennials. Disappointment made me doubt God. I told God I hated Him during that season. At the time, I meant it. I now know that one of the reasons I loved John was because I loved the God who lived inside of him. When I let John go, I let God go too.

Letting go of John didn't take the desire for companionship away. It made me want it all the more. I felt hollow. I didn't welcome the loneliness but that void later brought me into a new relationship with the Lord.

John brought incredible good into my life. God used John and his family as protection over me. The year after I broke up with John was lonely and terrifying. But, John's family protected me even when we were apart. His dad once told me that he and his wife woke up several times in the middle of the night feeling prompted by the Holy Spirit to pray for me. And in the darkness of night, they would climb out of bed, get on their knees, and pray.

I know that in God's goodness, John's parents interceded for me on the nights I needed it the most. I didn't know it then, but I had two warriors fighting for me. I thought I was alone, tossing and turning in my sleep. But, I wasn't.

I feared I was invisible to God, but He still saw me. Even though I turned my back on Him, He was still protecting and wooing me through the prayers of His warriors.

QUESTIONS FOR THE MEANWHILE:

1. What goodbyes have you made in the *Meanwhile?*

2. What relationships have seemed so right in certain areas but not right in other areas? What does God want you to do about each one?

3. Is there someone whose advice you listen to ahead of God's advice?

4. What unmet expectation(s) have you experienced?

5. How do you handle disappointment? What have been healthy ways you have coped with it and what have been unhealthy?

6. Who do you blame when life doesn't go as planned? How have you sought answers rather than blame?

Scripture to Memorize:

"For he satisfies the longing soul, and the hungry soul he fills with good things." Psalm 107:9 ESV

Counselor's Corner

Self-Care Action Plan

All of us will experience loneliness and disappointment. When that happens I want you to know that you are beautiful, you are enough, you are worthy, and you are capable. Listen to your body and listen to your soul when they are speaking to you. Some days we need to slow down, rest and take extra good care of ourselves. Other days, we need to get outside and get moving.

Self-care is the intentional action one takes to care for one's mind, body and soul. When I have felt lost, lonely, confused or disappointed, self-care has become paramount. I have had to learn what types of life-giving activities I need for replenishment. One of these is getting around people, as my story earlier in this book illustrates. Another is to learn what we enjoy doing (big or small) and do more of it. My mom takes a weekly painting class as part of her self-care. Others splurge on a fancy dinner out or get their nails done. It looks different for everyone but a few things I enjoy include:

Self-Care Menu

MIND	BODY	SOUL
READ A BOOK	GO ON A WALK	ANTIQUE SHOPPING
LISTEN TO A PODCAST	STRETCH/DO YOGA	TALK WITH A FRIEND
WORK A PUZZLE	GET A MASSAGE	WRITE POETRY/ CREATE ART
PLAY A GAME	BUY NEW BODY LOTION	TAKE A DEEP BREATH; LET OUT A SIGH
WATCH A DOCUMENTARY	GET MORE SLEEP; or GET LESS SLEEP	LIGHT A CANDLE
VISIT A MUSEUM	EAT HEALTHY FOODS	SMILE
TAKE A CLASS	THROW A FRISBEE	PLAY WITH A DOG OR CAT
DO SOMETHING NEW	GET OUTSIDE; GARDEN; PLAY IN THE DIRT	READ A BOOK
READ AN ARTICLE; STUDY SOMETHING INTERESTING	TAKE A BIKE RIDE	TRAVEL; SCOPE OUT NEW SCENERY
TURN OFF THE TV; ENJOY THE SILENCE	DANCE TO YOUR FAVORITE SONG (EVEN IF IN FRONT OF YOUR MIRROR)	JOURNAL OR PRAY
WRITE A QUOTE OR BIBLE VERSE ON YOUR MIRROR; MEMORIZE	BUY A NEW OUTFIT OR BUY A TREAT (ICE CREAM/LATTE)	CLEAN/DE-CLUTTER

Step One:

Now make a menu with three columns (Mind, Body and Soul). Beneath each column, list self-care ideas that come to mind. Be sure to include a range of activities based on cost as well as time. You may have a five-minute window and something on your list needs to fit. Keep this list nearby and on lonely or hard days, pick something to do. We will best care for others if we are taking care of ourselves. The Bible calls this loving others as we love ourselves (Leviticus 19:18; Mark 12:31). Even Jesus spent time in solitude with the Father.

MIND	BODY	SOUL

Step Two:

Now that you have made your menu, there are several other items needed for self-care. Think through your week ahead and then answer the questions below. This will complete your self-care action plan:

1. Who is one person you can call to connect with?

2. What is one activity you can share with someone else?

3. What is one outside activity you would enjoy?

4. What kind of exercise can you do for forty-five minutes?

5. What is one act of kindness you can do for a stranger?

6. Describe one healthy meal you can cook at home.

7. Pick something fun to do this week for at least thirty minutes.

8. Name one Bible verse you will meditate on.

9. Pick one song to listen to that lifts your spirits.

10. Name one friend, co-worker or family member you can love this week. How can you show them you care?

Chapter Six
"Me Too"

"We admitted we were powerless over alcohol— that
our lives had become unmanageable."
~Alcoholics Anonymous

H i, my name is Amanda Grace, and I'm addicted to pleasing people.
"Hi, Amanda Grace."

That's how the Alcoholics Anonymous meeting began that early March morning. It was my second semester of seminary. Before the meeting, I stepped out of my SUV and onto the cement. I tugged at my sweater, grabbed my less-than-hot thermos of coffee and rubbed my nose to make it warm. I was scared because this would be my first twelve-step meeting. I was in an Addictions and Counseling course as part of the 15 credit hours I had scrambled to sign up for earlier that December. As part of an assignment, we were asked to visit different twelve-step groups and write about our experiences. A.A. was my first of three groups.

I recited my lines before finding my way to the church basement where the A.A. meeting would be held. *Hi, I'm Amanda Grace, and I'm an alcoholic.* But I wasn't an alcoholic. I was addicted to food and to pleasing people. Since that wasn't what this group was for, I created another introduction. I didn't want the group members to think I was observing them. I didn't want my face to show judgment instead of acceptance. I walked toward the entrance of the church and my thoughts continued to swirl. *What if they think I'm an alcoholic too? What if my shaking hands reveal withdrawal instead of the chill outside?*

Stepping through the door of the church basement, I found shelter from the cold. I smelled the dark roasted coffee and saw two friendly faces. I asked one of them if this was the room for A.A. The woman's eyes, like pools of grace, answered me without a single word. They drew me in. She showed me to a seat and kept me company until the group began. I shifted uneasily in my blue plastic chair as the introductions began.

It was finally my turn to introduce myself. As I looked around the room, I said, "Hi, my name's Amanda Grace, and I'm addicted to pleasing people." The group members began to laugh, but I felt accepted. I had used humor as my crutch, but the admission was true. Relationships are not an addiction (as long as they are healthy); but pleasing people is. As I eased my back in the seat, the ice seemed to melt in the room.

While I listened to everyone in the circle introduce themselves, humility pressed me deeper into my chair. I was scared to breathe for fear it would interrupt the sacredness of the circle. Members were welcomed after each admission of setback and sin. The stories were raw and personal. As some of the men and women spoke, their hands shook. There were several experiences so near to death that they had smelled it. They knew what one more drink could mean. How brave it was for them to be there that morning to share.

I cried through the latter half of the A.A. meeting. I heard the hope and desperation in their voices. The realization that superheroes aren't real and none of us are invincible resonated. I wasn't addicted to alcohol, but we all longed for something greater, something to fill our soul and empty void. I heard Jesus in every story and saw Him in the eyes of the woman I had met at the door. For the first time in several months, I felt Him near. As I sat there, looking at the faces around the room, I realized I wasn't only addicted to food and people pleasing. I was addicted to control. It was my cocktail of longing and need to control that made my heart cry, "Me too," after everyone spoke.

At the end of the meeting, an older gentleman brought me a tissue and placed his hand upon my shoulder. I quietly said "Thank you" and asked how long he had been in A.A. meetings. He shook his white crowned head and said, "Forever, honey." As he turned to leave, he looked over his shoulder and seemed to contemplate his words. He looked me in the eyes and said, "We aren't that different, are we?"

I walked out of that A.A. meeting with a belly full of coffee and a heart full of perspective. My eyes were opened, and for the first time in a long time, I felt connected to the only Higher Power I knew. I also felt connected to every man and woman in that room through their honesty and humanity. I longed to wear eyes of grace like the woman I had met at the door, and I craved the ability to shamelessly share my pain instead of hiding behind my fig leaves.

Leaving the A.A. meeting that morning, I didn't feel so alone. I knew what it was like to fail at playing God and so did the men and women in that circle. We may have been addicted to different things but we each knew withdrawal and the feeling of being hollow. I was in seminary; we learned about God daily. Even so, I felt the presence of the Lord more in that A.A. meeting than I did between any walls of the classroom.

I had pulled up roots—physical and relational—to move from Texas to Colorado. Being uprooted made me feel out of control. My friends in that A.A. meeting knew what it was to be out of control. According to Gerald May, addiction is the human effort to quench desire. Yet nothing was meant to satisfy us outside of God. I was beginning to realize that my desire for control and my desire to play God were, in fact, addictions. And I failed every time I tried to sit on God's throne. That's a truth I should have learned from Adam and Eve in the Garden of Eden.[1] I do not know better than God, and I can't be perfect like Him.

In the *Weight of Glory*, C.S. Lewis wrote of human desire:

> "It would seem that our Lord finds our desires not too strong, but too weak. We are half-hearted creatures, fooling about with drink and sex and ambition when infinite joy is offered us, like an ignorant child who wants to go on making mud pies in a slum because he cannot imagine what is meant by the offer of a holiday at the sea. We are far too easily pleased."

Addiction is the counterfeit cure for fear, control, disappointment, and sadness, all of which can occur in the *Meanwhile*. We fool around with sex, drink and ambition because we seek instant gratification instead of infinite joy. Why sacrifice our wills and desires for the joy God offers when alcohol, food, and people pleasing offer a quicker remedy? I sought satisfaction in diets and thin arms, but reaching my goal weight never quenched.

I was one of those half-hearted creatures C.S. Lewis talked about. In some ways, I always have been. I sought comfort with control. I manipulated my class schedule, my plans and the vision I had for my future. I tried to wrap myself up in a tiny impenetrable box of control where reality couldn't touch me. I was desperate to feel better.

It was a Saturday night in Denver and some friends from seminary invited me to dinner and a movie. In recent weeks, I had chosen the ineffective path of isolation. But, that wasn't working so I decided to give socializing a chance.

I met my friends for dinner at one of the girls' houses. Despite the chill outside, I felt a tinge of peace. I was laughing for the first time in quite some time. We sat in a circle and laughed over homemade cornbread and pumpkin soup. The blazing fire melted my icy heart. I felt a bit more contented as I settled into a plush armchair. *Maybe life isn't over*, I thought. *Maybe there is hope and I can make friends and a life here.* I had been wearing my pain like it was my favorite knitted sweater. But as the conversation continued and the fire crackled, I relaxed. The movie theatre was a block up the street, and as I walked briskly to stay warm, I thought, *Maybe the gloom has finally lifted.*

But a few scenes into the movie, something happened. I felt an all too familiar sting of loneliness. I felt invisible and hollow. I shouldn't have been surprised because I had been isolating myself for a few weeks, but I was. I panicked. My mind flipped through Colorado memories like pictures in a slideshow. I saw how out of control my eating disorder had become (crazier than it had ever been). I saw every disconnection I had created. I heard every goodbye I had made. I watched as each unmet expectation flashed before my eyes.

I was overcome by fear and anxiety. I felt paralyzed. I started to sweat and my heart began to race when I realized this same feeling had initially triggered the panic when I crossed state lines. Rock bottom had come as a snowball effect. But, not yet feeling known, misunderstood and unseen—those feelings had been there all along.

And that's where Satan wants us: isolated and alone. As I sat in the movie theatre, surrounded by friends who truly cared, all I could think about were the nights I laid in bed, afraid of the shadows on the walls. Satan likes to cover us in shame and lies. And that's what he did. I've never been more terrified.

What is wrong with you? Can't you let go of the disappointment? I asked myself. When the movie finally ended, I felt sick. I nearly sprinted down the icy streets to get back to my car where I could hide my tears and calm my queasy stomach. Elizabeth was going to stay the night, because I was scared to be alone.

As I drove down the highway, my thoughts raced faster than the spinning car wheels. I thought I was losing my mind. I turned my music up loud to gain focus to safely make it home. My vision got blurry in the emotion. Falling snow covered my windshield. As I glanced to my left, I saw the reflective lights of the median. *Maybe if I run my car into it, someone would pay attention,* I thought. *If I were actually bleeding, someone would know I was hurting. And if I were lying in a hospital bed, someone would have to take care of me.*

Satan's schemes are terrifying. Even though I logically knew that, the voice of Darkness seeped in. As my headlights shone on the car ahead, I snapped into reality. *Don't be foolish, Amanda Grace,* I told myself. *You've got to get home. This must be what those men and women in A.A. were talking about—the moment you realize your life has become unmanageable.*

I eventually pulled into my garage and ran up the stairs. I wanted to kiss the ground. I had never felt Satan's cold hands so tightly around my neck before. Loneliness and pain thumped so loudly in my ears, I couldn't hear myself think. The voice of Darkness nudged again but then I heard a voice much louder, the voice of Love and Light. "It's going to be okay Amanda Grace."

Someone knocked on my door. I breathed a sigh of relief. It was Elizabeth.

The voice of Darkness is a convincing one. The Bible tells the truth: the thief comes to steal, kill and destroy (John 10:10, NIV). While Satan may be stealthy, I was the one who left my front door open. I had allowed my emotions to drown out Truth. I let sadness tell me that God was no longer good. I listened when desperation said life was hopeless.

That night was the wake-up call I needed to get help to know God again. I called a Christian Counselor the next week and began doing the hard work it takes to heal. I never thought about harming myself again after that night. I might not have called God my "friend" then. But He was and He is. It was His voice of Love and Light that protected me that night.

Satan wants to get us alone. Fight the desire to isolate. This doesn't mean you tell everyone what's going on inside of you, but always have one or two people you can be honest with. Engage with friends over time. Then use discernment to choose whom to share your heart with.

Shame and depression can only be fought in community.

The "perfect child" had become desperate and frantic. I thought I could do life alone. I thought I could control everything. But I couldn't. The men and women in that A.A. meeting were one drink away from ending their lives. I was one bad decision away from destroying my own. We sought to fill our emptiness rather than turning to the only one who can fill it: God with the help of those He sends our way.

I questioned God's goodness when I experienced disappointment. But God's goodness is not confined to circumstance. His love for us is unchanging. He will show us what to do in every situation, good or bad. The choice is ours. I chose wrongly by turning my back on God but as I learned in Alcoholics Anonymous, He was able to eventually restore me (in the deepest of His graces) to sanity.

Special Note to Readers:

If you or someone you know is experiencing any type of addiction, self-harm or suicidal thoughts, call a trusted pastor, mentor or Christian counselor. These thoughts and actions are signs help is needed. No matter what you believe otherwise, harming yourself will not fix anything. It may seem to release the pain or numb momentarily but in the end, it will hurt you more. Harming yourself prolongs the feelings and difficulties. There is hope in Jesus Christ and I pray that in Him, you can find freedom. Please be sure you take care of yourself. You are worth it.

*Call the National Suicide Prevention Lifeline at 1-800-273-TALK (8255) if you or someone you know needs help.

QUESTIONS FOR THE MEANWHILE:

1. If you were to attend an AA meeting, to what would you say you are addicted? (e.g. good grades, perfection, success, people-pleasing)

2. What is the desire behind each addictive behavior? What are healthy ways to cope and behave instead? How can these behaviors meet the purpose of each of your desires?

3. How have you attempted to play God? Why doesn't this work?

4. Describe a time of desperation and what you did about it. In what way(s) was this a healthy or unhealthy way of coping?

5. What has God taught you through walking through times of desperation? Who in your life can help you remember (and live) these truths?

Counselor's Corner

How-To Handle the Blues

If you find yourself feeling sad or depressed, here are three exercises to help:

1. Be Gentle with Yourself.

    b. Re-visit the self-care action plan you created in Chapter Five. Choose items from your self-care menu in step one to practice and answer the questions found in step two. Don't rush through these activities. Go slow and show yourself the same grace you would give someone else as you complete step one and two.

    c. Speak words of love and kindness to yourself, the type of thoughtful words God speaks to you. What would you say to a friend or colleague who was hurting or wrestling? Speak these same words of comfort and encouragement to yourself.

2. Do the Next Best Thing.

    When you feel like you're in a fog, narrow your focus. Don't look at the long list of to-dos; simply focus on doing the next best thing. There were days I had enough energy for washing one load of clothes, nothing more. Victory began with getting out of bed. That was all.

3. Receive God's love.

    "God has taken my hand because I don't know the way, I don't know where I am going. He is my personal guide, directing and shepherding me through rocky and scary country. He is right here to show me what roads to take, making sure I do not fall into the ditch. He is and will do all of these things for me—sticking with me, not leaving me for a second." (Isaiah 42:16, THE MESSAGE).

4. Meditate on Scripture (even if you're mad at God)

    a. Write verses on your mirror, on your hand, or on a pad of paper and carry them around. Read them over throughout the day. Let God's truth soak over you.

    b. Use Appendix A for a starter list of verses to meditate on.

    c. Meditate on Psalm 46:10 in the following sequence:

        I. Be.
        II. Be still.
        III. Be still and....
        IV. Be still and know.
        V. Be still and know that....
        VI. Be still and know that I am.
        VII. Be still and know that I am God.

Chapter Seven
Desire

"No change of job, no increased income, no new
home, no new electronic device, or no new spouse is
going to make things better inside of you."
~Matt Chandler - *The Explicit Gospel*

It is no secret that Millennials want a lot out of life. I think that's
our human predicament: wanting. We want to change the world,
we want to be loved and we want to be significant. To be human is to
know such desires. God created us this way. The trick is knowing what
to do with our wanting.

The experience of unfulfilled desire is like being parched and
longing for a glass of water. The difference in a goal and a desire is that
goals are often autonomous while desire is communal. We can't fulfill
desires on our own. We need the help of the Father. Certain desires are
accomplished with our effort. Others are only fulfilled in surrender.
For instance, if we desire success, we might put in the extra hours at
work or take a certification course. In His providence, God will be the
one to open the right doors and make the right connections.

Desire is a good thing. It's what makes us a heart-beating human.
We might crave wealth, understanding, good health, and so on. None
of these are innately bad. Misplaced desire is where we get ourselves
into trouble because the trajectory makes all the difference. We can lose
sight of the Giver if we focus too much on the gift. If we hoard desire
like stolen sweets, we run the risk of hurting ourselves—and others.
Desire is best held in His hands, not ours.

God may or may not give us the desires of our heart. That family member might not be healed, that relationship may not mend and no child may come. Those are precious things to mourn. But God is not cruel. He is redemptive. One day, (even if not on this earth) God will redeem you and personally wipe away every tear you have cried (Revelation 21:1-4). That doesn't make it hurt less but it does give us hope. Unfulfilled desire is an indicator that we are citizens of heaven.

We live in a fallen world and there will be pain. The Lord understands (Hebrews 2:17-18, 4:14-16). He can be trusted with our wanting. He rises *up* off of His throne for you. Literally. Close your eyes and picture it. He longs to be gracious to you and He rises to show you compassion (Isaiah 30:18).

The Message translation of this same verse says: "But God's not finished...He takes the time to do everything right—everything." He loves you and is for you—more than anyone ever could be. There will be things we don't understand. There will be questions without answers. But, God is always doing something.

It's a hard thing to wait. We all want the next best thing. I try to be content, but I want it all now. I don't know if discontentment from delayed gratification is in our DNA or if it was the way we were raised. Dr. Jeffrey Arnett explains in his article, "Oh, Grow Up!" that:

"High hopes in emerging adulthood are remarkably widespread (Arnett, 2000, 2004). Across ethnic groups and social classes, American emerging adults almost universally believe that eventually life will be kind to them. Even if life is not going so well right now—and often it is not, what with job changes, love upheavals, and financial difficulties— eventually all will be well. Everyone will find a job that provides a satisfying identity fit, pays well, and maybe even does some good in the world. Everyone will eventually find not just a mere flesh and blood marriage partner but a 'soul mate.'"

I want to matter to people. I want to be seen and heard. I want to be needed, and I want to be loved. The Bible affirms these desires. God has designed us to live in community, each of us helping another. My desire for significance is what led me to counseling, and my desire to be known is the reason I cherish relationships.

I have never been more aware of my wanting than now. I long for the next stage in life because I feel stuck in the one I'm in. I fear everyone has moved on and left me behind. Desire looks and feels different for each of us, but the thirst is the same. At the heart of all our desires is a longing for God.

Millennials are not unique in this way. Every good desire is founded on a characteristic of God we are longing for.

Instead of seeing desire as a vehicle God could use to draw me closer to Him and to His people, I blamed Him for withholding good from me. He was doing nothing of the kind. It's not in His character. God is not a God of scarcity. He is a God of fullness. He offers fullness of life, of joy, and of Him (John 10:10; Colossians 2:10).

An important note: Just because God gives to someone else does not mean He is taking from you or me. If we believe so, we run the risk of losing sight of His goodness altogether.

Desire for Success

My sister moved to California to chase her dreams at the University of Southern California. Lindsey has wanted to be an actress since childhood. She was born to entertain. When I was ten and Lindsey was eight, our family traveled to Walt Disney World. We attended the Hoop-Dee-Doo Musical Revue, a performance consisting of an emcee, can-can dancers and a syndicated bar brawl. It was quite thrilling for our little eyes and minds.

Halfway through the show, the emcee walked out into the audience in his stirrups and cowboy hat to pick a volunteer to assist him. He chose Lindsey. Lindsey jumped out of her chair and pranced toward the stage excitedly. It wasn't five minutes later that Lindsey had the entire audience laughing.

Desire took Lindsey halfway across the country. She grew up playing with fake microphones and dreaming of one day being on stage. Lindsey wants to bring people joy through entertainment. To chase her dreams, Lindsey had to close the doors on her other options. She would no longer live close to family nor would she attend the family alma mater.

Lindsey began to feel like the black sheep of the family when her life started to look different from all of ours.

But she wasn't.

Lindsey learned that the Los Angeles culture was unlike the small town feel she had experienced growing up in suburban Texas. Lindsey wondered if her desire to find success was worth it, even while working to become a reporter at an esteemed television network.

She explained, "Though there were days I did things I had always dreamt of, there was still a nagging doubt and fear that I might never achieve the success I yearned for both professionally and personally."

Lindsey found herself wondering if she made the right decision in moving to Los Angeles. Would God bring her success in her career as an entertainer or a reporter? Would He open the doors for her to get in front of the camera? And after success is found professionally, would she get to start a family and live the cul-de-sac lifestyle?

Desire for Intimacy

Desire is not one-size-fits-all. For Lindsey, it's the desire for an entertainment career that keeps her thirsty. For my friend Rachel, it's the desire for intimacy and family. For others, it's a desire for both career and home success.

Rachel and I met two years after I moved to Denver while at a St. Patrick's Day brunch complete with green food dye. As transplants from the south, we found a friend in one another. Rachel and I are both counselors, enjoy a good meal, and have similar desires. We spent many Saturday mornings together making green smoothies and fresh vegetable omelets filled with the farmer's market goodies we had found that day.

When one of us had a bad day, we drove downtown to stand in line for salted Oreo® ice cream. We people-watched in front of the milk-can-shaped ice-cream shop. Conversation comes easily for us.

Rachel and I both long for marriage and a family of our own. We believe God reserved sex for marriage, and so, as we wait for a husband, we also wait for deeper intimacy. We know that "True Love Waits" but no one told us how long we'd be waiting. We remind each other of the good gift God gave in sexuality. We crave physical intimacy and know the struggle of waiting during this season of singleness. So we support one another as we prepare for marriage.

It's hard to remain pure for my husband, and as I've gotten older, it has only gotten more difficult. I've made mistakes along the way but I'm determined to love my future spouse in this way. Despite the difficulty, I remind myself of why I wait. Purity is for our protection, not for our punishment. We can protect the oneness we will share with our husbands with our current decisions.

Some of us have made poor sexual decisions. Please remember that even when we make mistakes, God still loves us deeply and is always in the business of redemption. He calls us clean, redeemed, and new. Don't let Satan tell you otherwise. He is a liar, after all.

My parents gave Lindsey and me three rules to help us navigate the physical side of relationships. They're called "The Three Nothing's": Nothing laying down, nothing without clothes on and nothing below the neck. I have learned four other guidelines over the years. First, nothing good happens after midnight. Second, alcohol only complicates things. Third, our hearts are just as important to protect as our bodies. And lastly, date a man who protects both your heart and your body.

Three books that have helped me navigate dating and waiting are:

How to Get a Date Worth Keeping,

Meaning of Marriage and

Who's Picking me up from the Airport?

How to Get a Date Worth Keeping offers practical advice on dating in general. Author Henry Cloud encourages the reader to get their numbers up by making a list of all the men they know to get to know different types of people. This helps us know what we're looking for.

Cloud's dating tools are best lived out when read in tandem with Tim Keller's, *The Meaning of Marriage.* Keller affirms the goal of marriage is holiness, not happiness. He shows how to choose a Godly mate.

Cindy Johnson's *Who's Picking Me Up from the Airport* is a humorous and uplifting read. Through sharing her story and others, Johnson invites readers to celebrate single life for what it is: joyful and complicated. She makes us single girls feel a little less alone.

It doesn't matter our life stage, our age or our marital status; desire never goes away. A married couple I know is the only couple in their small group without children. Their parents are starting to drop hints about what they hope their grandchildren will call them. This couple is having a hard time getting pregnant. I can only imagine the pain at reading another negative pregnancy test: the anticipation each month that's met with heart-breaking disappointment.

You aren't alone in your longing. Think about your deepest desire. Name it and ask God, "Lord, I can't hold [this desire] any longer without your help. I long for [it] to be fulfilled. Is there something I can do to help that happen? Help me to trust in Your goodness and to believe that You withhold no good thing from me. You alone are the greatest gift I could ever be given. Let me rest assured in this today."

QUESTIONS FOR THE MEANWHILE:

1. What would you name as your deepest desires? Answer it this way: "If a miracle came tonight that changed something in your life what would you experience when you woke up tomorrow morning?" Whatever you answered may be your deepest desire(s).

2. In what ways has this desire gone unfulfilled? What might God want you to do next about it?

3. What is the root of your desire? (i.e. you're created that way by God, what is the reason for it?)

4. How have you tried to satisfy this desire outside of God?

5. What are godly ways to seek success and significance? What avenues can bring negative attention to God?

6. Now take some time to sit and pray to the Lord. Think about the root of your desire and ask God to show you people and actions to fill the void you're experiencing. What aspect of His character can you hold onto in your longing? See the chart in the Counselor's Corner for help in naming an attribute.

Counselor's Corner

The Communicable and Incommunicable Attributes of God

God has communicable (traits we can possess) and incommunicable (traits only He can possess) attributes. While this list is not exhaustive, start with this sample list of attributes. Which attribute do you need to cling to? To imitate? To live in light of?

COMMUNICABLE	INCOMMUNICABLE
SPIRIT	ETERNAL
THOROUGHLY LOVING	CAN SEE OUR FUTURE
SELFLESS	NOT BOUND BY TIME
EMPATHIZES	WANTS THE VERY BEST FOR US
PERSONAL	INFINITE
GOOD	IMMUTABLE (NEVER-CHANGING)
HOLY	IMMANENT (NEARNESS)
LOVE	TRANSCENDENT
TRUTHFUL	OMNIPRESENT
WISE	OMNISCIENT
MERCIFUL	OMNIPOTENT
KIND	SOVEREIGN

Chapter Eight
Envy

"I want an Oompa Loompa now!"
~Veruca Salt - *Willy Wonka & the Chocolate Factory*

Comparison is not the only thief of joy. Envy has sticky fingers too. *I want a Barbie!* Four-year-old me cried in the middle of a childhood birthday party I attended. I became a puddle of tears as I kicked and screamed. My mom graciously took me by the hand and led me outside the party room. As I had been eating my cake, the birthday girl opened my favorite thing in the world: a Barbie doll. I assumed, as any four-year-old might, that if she got a new Barbie doll, then surely I would too. My birthday was right around the corner and my mom had bought me the same exact doll. It just wasn't time to open it.

That behavior is appropriate for a four-year-old. Not so much for us. Though we no longer throw overt tantrums we may still wonder when it'll be our turn. "When will my dream job come along?" "Why haven't I found purpose?" "Why does she get to stay home with her kids?"

A few months after my battle with the voice of Darkness, I got a phone call from my dear friend's boyfriend. He would be proposing in a month and invited me to the engagement party. I might have been in a low spot but I wanted to be there to celebrate Jane. They were two of my favorite people to be around, and it was right for me to celebrate with them. Even after college, Jane traveled to Colorado every year on my birthday to make sure I felt loved. She is one of the best friends I know.

Doing the right thing when hard, leads to better things. The plane ride was worth seeing the look on Jane's face. She had no idea what was coming! The day before my trip, I was in my bedroom packing. I felt like a Ping-Pong ball being hit between two sides of the table. On one end, I had immense joy for Jane and Tim, but on the other, I found myself longing. That little four-year-old cried, *what about me?*

I chose to make the weekend about Jane's happiness and not my discontentment. It was important I celebrate her and not sulk in self-pity or selfishness. With that in mind, I painted my nails a pale pink and packed the brightest outfit I owned—a yellow blouse and green shorts. I wanted to be cheerful for Jane. When the morning of the engagement party came, I got dressed, put on a sparkling necklace and pinned back my hair. I was going to celebrate well.

I said a prayer as I drove to the engagement party with a friend. *Lord, be present today. Give me the courage to turn my longing over to you for safekeeping. Let me love Jane well.*

We waited for about thirty minutes before Jane and Tim arrived. I went to the bathroom and breathed a few deeps breaths. When I feel overwhelmed or insecure, I run to the bathroom to talk to God and give myself a little pep talk. It's how I surrender my longing and my insecurity. I tell myself, *you are loved and you are seen. You feel lonely right now, but you're not alone. He sees you, and He hears you.*

A few minutes later, Jane and Tim came through the front door. Instantaneously, I got tears in my eyes. I was so happy for my sweet friend. Jane hugged her parents and began to scan the room. As she looked around, her eyes landed on me. She threw her arms around my neck. She began to cry. "I can't believe you're here!" She squealed. "I can't believe you came all this way." I couldn't have been happier that I had come. It was the best feeling in the world to celebrate her and feel so loved in return. There was no other place I would have rather been.

It's okay to feel sad and long for a Barbie Doll at times. What's not okay is to be selfish. Jeffery Arnett says transition and self-focus are two of the five hallmarks of the *Meanwhile*. Transition can exacerbate envy, the fear we lack something. Self-focus can rouse jealousy, the fear we will lose something. Whether the fear is rooted in loss or lack, the angst extends to bank accounts, the size of our homes, being a stay-at-home mom versus working outside of the home, vice versa, and more. A friend once told me she used to envy girls who had found their husbands. Now that she's engaged, she's jealous of those who got the exact wedding they wanted. The wanting never stops.

The Bible calls jealousy an idol. And a bossy idol it is. *"That's mine!"* it cries out. Every time I answer the cry, I have another mess to clean up. Envy extinguishes our ability to show empathy. I have countless stories to tell you that would prove that to be true.

At the root of all disorder is bitterness. I was the ugliest version of myself when I was bitter. I don't want to be known as the woman who has a hard time celebrating her friends. I don't want to be the four-year-old who had to be taken out of the birthday party. I want to be the woman who is tender, not bitter. The woman who can celebrate another without asking, "what about me?"

Choose the better way. God calls us to a love that does not seek self. Any time "What about me?" enters my mind I see a flashing yellow sign. There's a heart issue going on here. And if I follow the rabbit trail of that thought, it isn't going to end well. We all have trigger thoughts like that. What is yours?

I think of the older brother in the story of the Waiting Father. This older brother had done everything right. When his rebellious sibling came home after miles of bad decisions, he walked into the arms of a loving father. The Waiting Father greeted his son with celebration instead of rejection. He showered him with good clothes to wear and a fattened calf to eat. The older brother grew jealous. "Why can't I be celebrated when I've always done the right thing?" His father responded, "'Son, I am always with you. Everything I have is yours. It was right to celebrate and be glad, for this your brother was dead, and is alive; he was lost, and is found." (Luke 15:11-32, NIV.)

I am practicing the celebration of others. I don't want to refuse to celebrate the way the older brother did. After all, celebration is Biblical. It's God-given. We read dozens of stories about feasts and festivals, all declaring the glory of God. A friend once told me that she finds it easier to celebrate others if she takes the time to celebrate the good that God has done in her life. She says when we celebrate, we acknowledge and thank God for the good works He has set out for us to fulfill. If we reject the celebrations God has given us because we'd rather have something else, we reject God.

It is fitting to celebrate different people, in different seasons for different reasons. We're all worth celebrating as sons and daughters of the King. The Waiting Father has arms open-wide for all of us. He shows no favoritism. We need to show this same love for one another.

So, celebrate your friends. Take them out to dinner, buy them a thoughtful gift, or write them an encouraging note. My friend says it best: Worth and dignity are bred from celebration. Let's be thankful for the good in our lives so we can celebrate from an overflow, not a deficit, of heart.

God taught me something that weekend at the engagement party. He showed me something better than envy. He showed me loving-kindness and humility. God used the party as an opportunity to uproot the ugly and plant the loving. Had I chosen otherwise (as I have before) He wouldn't have had the chance to dig out the envy that needed pruning. I wouldn't have experienced the nearness of God had I chosen self-pity.

To this day, that engagement party is still my favorite memory with Jane. I smile as I think back to her excitement when she walked through the front door and found me in the crowd. Show up for the difficult. Learn to celebrate others well. Push through and lean in. Otherwise, we deprive God of the opportunity to do something good in us. I don't want to miss the embrace the Waiting Father has for me because I'm too upset about the fattened calf someone else received.

QUESTIONS FOR THE MEANWHILE:

1. Who do you need to celebrate today? How can you do so?

2. In what ways is selfishness or bitterness spilling into your relationships?

3. How can you put yourself aside to celebrate others well?

4. I recognize I have a heart issue when I think, "What about me?" What question or thought warns you that your heart is on a dangerous track? By naming these thoughts, we can better choose how to act when they enter our mind.

5. What role does envy play in your life and relationships? Talk with God and ask God to give you love instead.

6. What is one thing you can celebrate the Lord doing in your life?

Counselor's Corner

Create a Thought Log

We behave and feel out of the way we think. For instance, if we think we are forgotten, we feel left behind and act as such. On the other hand, if we think we are loved, we feel accepted and act as though we are wanted. The Bible calls us to captivate our thoughts. The reason is the fact that our thinking controls everything. If we have pure thoughts, we'll have a healthier life. If we have bitter or distorted thoughts, we'll have a discontented life. In counseling, there is a progression called an A-B-C Triangle. A stands for Activating Event. B stands for Behavior and C stands for Consequence. Similarly, I believe in a T-F-A Triangle. T stands for Thought. F stands for Feeling. And A stands for Action. What is our goal in a given circumstance? On the day of Jane's engagement party, my goal was to be cheerful and content so I could celebrate my friend well. If those were my purposed feelings and action, what kinds of things did I need to be thinking? Using a thought log allows us to reframe our thoughts so that we can breed a healthier, more contented life. Below are some example thought transformations. Use the extra space to track your thoughts this week:

UNHEALTHY	HEALTHY
I'll be the only unmarried girl at the party this weekend.	Maybe there's someone new I can meet? Or there might be an old friend I can talk to.
I'm left behind.	There's no such thing. I'm in a different lane.
My friends have forgotten about me.	No they haven't. Look at the embrace Jane gave you. They still love you.

Chapter Nine
Indecision

"Paralysis is a consequence of
having too many choices."
~Barry Schwartz

The easiest decision I ever made was to become a counselor. I made
up my mind when I was thirteen. My youth group had gone
on a mission trip to Reynosa, Mexico, a border city south of the Rio
Grande. Our trip that week consisted of various activities including
construction and street evangelism. When my team's turn came for
street evangelism, we split off into twos and threes and headed down
the city streets.

The streets were sandy, and the air was heavy. Typically nervous to
do this type of thing, it felt safer in Mexico. The translator and I walked
door-to-door talking and listening to people. I loved it. I came alive
getting to connect with people who, though on the surface seemed
so different from me, were so similar to me. They wanted love and
acceptance like I did.

Toward the end of our week we had a free afternoon. I decided
to go sit on the steps of the chapel that lay on the outskirts of the
compound. The worship band was warming up for the service later
that evening. I began to think and pray. *I'm made for this,* I thought.
*I'm made to connect to people and to hear their stories. I've never felt more
alive. I'm going to be a counselor.*

A few months after that trip, our translator, Joann, came to visit our youth group. When my family and I walked into church that Sunday morning, I saw Joann standing against the windows outside the sanctuary. I ran up to her and gave her a big hug. Joann held my hands in hers and asked my mom and me to meet her after the service because she had a message she wanted to share with us. I was curious as to what it was.

After the service, we met in the hallway, and the three of us found a corner to talk. "I had a dream" she said, "and you were in it." She went on to say that she'd had a vision of me sitting in the middle of a circle of teenage girls and I was teaching them. That was the first of many confirmations of my calling.

I had felt called to be a counselor but after my first few counseling classes, I felt disenchanted. I thought counseling was my purpose. But studying to be a counselor was harder than I thought it would be. In every class I had to think about and talk about all the ways I didn't measure up. I honestly can't tell you how many times I had to answer the question, "How do you feel about that?" Every paper I wrote seemed to end with my dysfunction. I diagnosed my family of origin issues and even wrote a sexual autobiography. There was nothing left unturned. I felt overwhelmed.

The subjects we studied lacked lightness. I experienced depravity and pain in a way I never had before. I lost my innocence in the classroom. The real world was defined by the abuse, neglect and disorders I was learning about.

On Being a Therapist by Jeffrey Kottler describes how therapists are deeply influenced by their clients. One counselor shares, "You will face your most terrifying demons every week, and this takes its toll…you will see people when they are at their worst, and you will be expected to present yourself at your best. Every time."

Counselors have little margin of error. We can't afford bad-hair days or sick days. We must show up in perfect condition every time. Yes, we're human but people depend on us.

I felt called to be a counselor, but in the whirlwind of my first year of seminary and the weight of the counseling profession, I forgot. I got scared.

My family's mantra was "Dress for Success." So I chose my outfit carefully for my first client. As I jumped in my car and drove toward campus, I gave myself a pep talk. *You can do this.* I stepped out of my car and looked toward the double doors. *Here goes nothing,* I thought.

I met my client in the waiting room and led her back to our assigned room. I tried to act like I had done this a hundred times before. And yet, I fumbled through the intake and the paperwork. I choked over the word "psychotherapy." I smiled as though I was trying to calm her nerves, but I was calming my own. I looked up at the video camera that was recording our session and I glanced at the clock. *How is that possible?* Only ten minutes had passed.

I was a ticking time bomb sitting in the counselor's chair. I ran through all the questions I could think of and tried to remember what my professors had taught us. The sound machine outside our door hummed even louder. I glanced at the clock again. Only five more minutes had gone by. I was in agony. The voices in my head and the fear in my spirit grew louder.

I spent six weeks with clients that summer, and every session I had went like this first one. I thought, *What in the world am I doing? I must have heard God wrong. There is no way this is what He called me to. If it were, this would be easier, more enjoyable.*

I saw God through the lens of doubt I created instead of letting Him reveal Himself to me. I endured many sleepless nights that summer. I woke up in the middle of the night frantic, sweating, fearful God had forgotten about me. I felt lost and confused. Indecision settled in. *Should I stay in Colorado? Should I move home?*

I hit a wall when I got a voicemail from the counseling clinic: "Amanda Grace, you have a new client." I burst into tears. I could barely handle the four clients I had.

I was at a conference in Michigan when I received the call. I put my phone away before walking downstairs for dinner. In the lobby was a girl I had met earlier in the day. She had a Frisbee in her hand and she looked like she needed a friend. She walked up smiling and asked if I wanted to throw the Frisbee before dinner. Typically I would say "yes," but I felt no compassion or empathy. Instead of choosing the life-giving option in loving her, I selfishly chose me. I told her I was busy before dinner but that I'd see her later. She gave me an understanding smile and graciously said, "That's okay," before turning and walking away.

What am I doing? I thought. *That was so rude of me. You're not busy. You're just busy being self-consumed.* The conference ended two days later, and as I sat at the airport waiting for my plane, I decided I couldn't go back to Colorado. I couldn't keep doing this. I was forcing it. I wanted out and quickly. I emailed my clinical director right then, and told her I was quitting practicum. I needed to stop seeing clients. A week later, I was making the trip back home to Texas. I left a stack of boxes in my apartment packed and ready to move. I wasn't planning on returning.

QUESTIONS FOR THE MEANWHILE:

1. What has indecision looked like in your life? How have you questioned what you previously thought to be true?

2. To whom or what did you turn to for answers when confused? How do you feel about the answers you chose? What would you do differently if you had a do-over?

3. Have you experienced feeling stuck? How and when?

4. How have you handled, or could you handle, a crossroads in your life? What actions and answers has God provided to you during a decision you needed to make or a direction you needed to take?

Scripture to Memorize:

"Good and upright is the Lord; He guides the humble in what is right and teaches them His way…. All His ways are loving and faithful…He will instruct [me] in the way chosen for [me]. My eyes are ever on the Lord…. Guard my life and rescue me, let me not be put to shame, for I take refuge in you. May integrity and uprightness protect me, because my hope is in you"
(Psalm 25: 8-10; 12; 20-21, NIV).

Chapter Ten
Grace

"If you want God's grace, all you need is
need, all you need is nothing."
~Tim Keller

That first weekend home, I helped run Outback Texas, a Christian camp for parents/teens and husbands/wives at our family's farm in Brenham. I had long loved camp ministry but as we drove to the farm I wanted to be anywhere but there. Even though I was home physically, I felt unsettled.

God seemed silent. But once again, I was projecting my fear on Him instead of letting Him place His peace on me.

I didn't want people to ask me questions. I just wanted to enjoy my time at home alone, without people around. My advice fell on deaf ears. I chose isolation over connection.

The camp weekend consisted of various talks, low ropes activities, small group discussions, and worship. Despite the sunshine outside, I felt gray and stormy inside. Sitting under the big white tent listening to people sing about how much they loved God was not the place I wanted to be. I had chosen better at Jane's engagement party. I was not choosing well now.

I hid in my parent's room much of the weekend. I didn't want people to gawk at the train wreck I had become. These people knew my family; they knew me as the perfect child. I didn't want them to see how confused and unhappy I had become.

I heard a knock on the door. My dad walked in. "Would you share your testimony at lunch today? We need someone to talk about what God has done in their life and what He means to them."

Of course I would mind, I thought to myself. Before I could open my mouth to respond, a tear fell down my cheek. *I usually jump at the chance to talk about how much I love God but right now, it feels too hard. How can I tell people how good God is when I've been questioning Him all year long?*

I looked up at my dad through blurry tears and said "No," with the sass of a teenage girl.

He seemed surprised. "I'll find someone else," he said as he walked out of the room and shut the door.

Who have I become? I thought. My anger was scaring me, and I know it scared my family and those around me. I had hit rock bottom before. I thought I was past that. I thought I was in the clear. Music reverberated up the hill to the farmhouse where I hid. I wanted to shut it all out and run away from this Jesus club. I didn't want to hear their singing or see their smiles. I felt trapped.

My concerned parents wanted me to pray with one of the women at the camp. I obliged. As I sat there with Lisa, her blue eyes comforted me. I felt safe with her, and despite my anger, I let the tears fall freely as I wept in her arms inside the prayer tent. I may not have wanted to share my testimony, but I did want to feel better.

The last day of camp was Sunday, and it happened to be April Fool's Day. I sure did feel like a fool. I had moved my whole life to Colorado to chase the calling I believed God had given me. But the moment I felt disappointment, I blamed Him.

God, where are you? Where did You go? One of the men who attended Outback that weekend chose to be baptized. I stood on the shore of the pond a few feet from my mom and watched as my dad stepped into the murky water and grabbed the hand of the man being baptized. As I stood there watching my heart began to flutter; it felt like it was going to fly out of my chest. I knew it was God speaking.

There is no way I am getting baptized, Lord. This wasn't how I planned it. I'm not doing this today. I don't even like you. As I looked at my feet, two butterflies began to swarm around me. I tried to ignore them but the beating grew louder.

I looked to my mom and walked towards her. "Do you think Dad would baptize me too?" I asked. Tears filled her eyes, and she put her hand on my shoulder. "Of course he would," she said. When the man got out of the water, my dad asked the crowd if anyone else would like to be baptized. I stepped forward, and he looked at me with loving, grace-filled eyes, like the woman I had met in the A.A. meeting. I was terrified to admit where I had been. But everyone looked at me with such compassion. I was thoroughly accepted.

I began to share my story. I told everyone that I had been so angry with God because I was disappointed and disillusioned with how life had turned out. I wept and shook as I stood next to my dad on that shore. Looking at the crowd one last time before we went into the water, I wanted this moment to be the one God would use to heal me.

My dad went ahead of me into the pond and reached back for my hand. I felt my feet sink deep in the mud as I waded out into the water to join him. He put his arm around my back and said "Amanda Grace, I baptize you in the name of the Father, the Son, and the Holy Spirit." I came out of the water refreshed. I wasn't healed instantly, but something had changed. I realized I needed God, and the lesson of grace was cemented. God's love washed over me in the cold water that day.

I had planned to be baptized at the end of seminary as a symbol of all I had learned and done. The view I had of baptism had little to do with God and everything to do with me. But, as it should be, my actual baptism had nothing to do with how good or perfect I was. It had everything to do with God's love. In His grace, He met me in my mess.

I had wondered where God went but I was the one who had abandoned Him. He had been there the whole time, patiently wooing me. He was the Waiting Father, standing there with arms open-wide, anticipating my return. I learned the full meaning of my new name. Amanda means "worthy of love" and Grace means "unmerited favor." Ann Voskamp says, "Grace doesn't ever negate transformation—but always initiates it." I still felt confused after my baptism, but there was something new: hope. I decided that day to trust and follow Jesus despite any fear that may come. I chose to give God my heart and life, even though it still terrified me to do so.

My parents and I drove home after camp. For the first time in a long time, I slept through the night without a nightmare or a cold sweat.

I still needed to make a decision about staying in Colorado or returning home. I made flow charts and pro and con lists to sort through my options. I ended up with a six-page document. I prayed and I listened. I asked God which way to go and I asked Him what His best was for me.

Later in the week, I heard a still, small voice as I sat at my desk pouring over the lists. The voice (although inaudible) sounded familiar. I had heard it the day I got baptized and on the chapel steps when I was called. I heard God say, "You're not done yet. You need to go back to Colorado." I heard God as a nudge in my spirit. It was loud and clear. I felt a tinge of peace. I had to go back.

I was scared being back in Denver would hurt like it had before. I didn't know what was to come. I glanced out the car window as my mom drove me to the airport at the end of the summer. A billboard caught my eye. "Come to Life," it said. And as I glanced again, it was a picture of the Rocky Mountains.

QUESTIONS FOR THE MEANWHILE:

1. For what decision do you need direction? Read God's Word (The book of Proverbs is a good place to start) and listen to God. Include some time of silence as you ask God to speak to you. Pay attention to His nudge.

2. Learning to hear God's voice happens over time. He will speak to each of us differently, in quiet or loud ways. Describe how this has happened for you. How does God speak to you? How can listening for Him become a regular practice?

3. If God gave you a new name what would it be?

4. How have you experienced second chances?

5. What do you need to be washed clean of today?

6. Describe what new life looks like for you. Today, walk in assurance that God has made all things new.

PART THREE
BECOMING ROOTED

"'It doesn't have many roots,' I say. 'Not yet,'
she says. 'That will come.'"
-Allyson Condie - *Reached*

Chapter Eleven
Trust

"For what does the Scripture say? 'Abraham believed
God, and it was counted to him as righteousness.'"
Romans 4:3

I walked up the stairs of my Colorado apartment and set my bags
down. I was scared to be back in Denver but I chose to trust the Lord
who called me back. I was learning what it meant to believe God. The
way Abraham did.

There on my nightstand was a note. It was from Elizabeth.

"And he arose and came to his father. But while he was still a long
way off, his father saw him and felt compassion, and ran and embraced
him and kissed him. And the son said to him, 'Father, I have sinned
against heaven and before you. I am no longer worthy to be called your
son.' But the father said to his servants, 'Bring quickly the best robe,
and put it on him, and put a ring on his finger and shoes on his feet.
And bring the fattened calf and kill it, and let us eat and celebrate. For
my son was dead, and is alive again; he was lost and is found." (Luke
15:11-32; NIV).

Welcome back.

I touched my fingertips to the page and closed my eyes. I was
coming home, not to the mountains, but to the arms of the Waiting
Father. A good Father I could trust.

"I'm not sure I can do this," I told Dianne, a dear woman who suggested I take a gratitude journey and use Ann Voskamp's book, *One Thousand Gifts* as my guide. It sounded so trite, gratitude. How could gratitude teach me to trust and hope again? Despite my disbelief, I agreed. After all, if nothing else had made me contented up to this point, I might as well give gratitude a try.

I told my mentor Melonie about the gratitude dare I had received, and she and I decided to walk through it together. Melonie had been my mentor throughout my entire time in Colorado and had become like family to me. Melonie walks with God in a genuine, deep way and she walks beside me (to this day) gently and intentionally. Isn't that the way of God? He brings people beside us at the time we need them.

Melonie and I met almost weekly for three years. Melonie became my safe haven. I would show up on her doorstep with puffy cheeks, red eyes and a disheveled ponytail. No matter my messy appearance, she opened the door and welcomed me in every time. I learned through her love that I didn't need to dress to impress after all.

We spent many days in her living room drinking peppermint tea and sharing open Bibles, open journals and open hearts. Melonie fought for me when I lost the strength to throw a punch. She told me she would stand in the gap for me when I felt hopeless. She never gave up on me.

Life hadn't turned out the way I expected but better things were coming. Counselors will tell you depression happens for all kinds of reasons. Mine came from ingratitude. I blamed God for every unmet expectation. I shook my fists at Him as though happiness in life was my right. I was spoiled. All the while God was offering me joy on a platter. I rudely turned from it.

I think Melonie knew I needed the discipline of gratitude. I needed to learn to offer a "sacrifice of thanksgiving." Ann Voskamp says it best in *One Thousand Gifts*: "We give thanks to God not because of how we feel but because of who He is."

In her book, Ann Voskamp tells the story of her gratitude journey and how she started to write down things she was thankful for every day, until she reached 1,000. She started to see more clearly when she started counting.

I heeded to the challenge and started to count. My thanking started out with small things:

1. *Smiling at a stranger.*
2. *The green light that let me be on time for class.*
3. *Getting a new friend's phone number.*

I learned that the Bible calls thank offerings a sacrifice because it's a choice and it takes discipline. I still had moments of loneliness and doubt, but I was learning to thank God, even during those moments. I thanked Him for the chill in the air, for the plane that left on time and for the chance to go hiking.

As the days went on, I noticed something. Instead of waking up apathetically, I woke up expectantly. I expected to see God. I expected Him to show me something good. I was starting to see. As I continued counting, I was beginning to trust God again.

I was no longer looking through a lens of discontentment; I was seeing through a lens of contentment. Gratitude propelled me toward God while ingratitude had repelled me from Him. I hadn't been grateful enough for my life. There were many with far worse circumstances that were more thank-filled than I.

It didn't matter as much that it was sub-zero temperatures in Denver or that I wasn't sure how the story would end. What mattered was letting a snowflake fall on my finger, one that looked nothing like the others. What mattered was there was a snow sweeper cleaning my apartment pathway, which made me feel cared for (and saved me from the cold).

I continued to count until I reached 1,000. It took a year. Some days the thanking was easy, and other days it was painful. But even when I struggled, I always found something to thank God for. No gift was too small to see or to count. I learned that as I counted, the gifts didn't get larger, my awareness for the gifts did.

72. *Spontaneously leaving class early to get chocolate chip pancakes at IHOP with Elizabeth.*

73. *A field of gold and leaves you want to drink.*

74. *Being able to see.*

75. A mile-high bubble bath with lavender sea salts.

76. The deer that pranced in front of me on the trail.

Voskamp says, "Life change comes when you accept life with thanks and ask for nothing to change." At the end of that year I no longer sat in fear, I woke up trusting. God had used gratitude to melt my icy heart.

I woke up one morning and watched the light bask the room. I felt different, new. I had pushed away the cloak of darkness. I was free. Apathy had been replaced with energy.

I got out of bed and started to thank God. What began as a sacrifice was now a healthy routine. I walked to the kitchen to make myself a cup of coffee and I thanked God. *God, thank you for waking me up early this morning, thank you for this robe keeping me warm, thank you for the morning light that kissed my face.*

Isaiah 26:3 tells us that if we keep our minds steadfast on the Lord, He will keep us in perfect peace, because we trust Him. I had to learn to trust in God again. It was gratitude that helped me do that. Ann Voskamp says, "No one receives the peace of God without giving thanks to God. Thankfulness is the deep, contented breath of Peacefulness." Gratitude was the vehicle God used to bring me to peace and joy. This didn't come overnight though. It took about a year to count, learn to pray and learn to read the Bible again. It took even longer to feel completely free—almost two years. So, go slow. The melting of a heart takes time even if God's responsiveness and tending doesn't.

I had to learn how to pray and read the Bible again. I started by telling God it was hard to spend time with Him. That was my version of prayer at the time. I just focused on telling God the truth. I grew up believing it was bad to be angry with God but I learned He's big enough to handle our anger. After all, it is a relationship.

If you're having a hard time praying to God or reading the Bible, find new ways to do both. Journal. Read other faith-filled books. The Chronicles of Narnia is a great read. I read a children's Storybook Bible.

I found freedom in reading children's books as an adult. They show us fresh truth.

Listen to podcasts. Tim Keller had three I listened to on repeat: "Praying our Fears," "Praying our Tears," and "Longing for Home."

Use short devotionals like *Jesus Calling*. Let your devotion times become bite-sized and manageable.

Read one chapter of the Psalms every day and soak in the words. Then move on to the Book of Proverbs.

Reading the Gospels helps you know the character of Jesus Christ and how to imitate Him. I would start in John.

My journal entries were the baby steps I needed to pray again. I found four steps crucial (and Biblical) in trusting God again. First, we must turn. **Turn** to face the Lord. Second, **remember**. We need to remember all He has done for us. Third, **pour**. We are invited to honestly pour our soul out to the Lord. And lastly, **repent**. Repent of what we have done and how we have strayed. He will always accept us back in.

I still have concerns, more than I'd like to admit. But, when I get scared God won't take care of me, I remember. I remember His character. It's more about Who He is than it is about what I experience. He took care of me so many times when I refused to see. Looking back, I can see that God sent Elizabeth to be with me that lonely night in Denver. And when I heard that knock on the door? It was Jesus asking to come in. These are moments I can be thankful for. Now, that I can see.

At the end of my gratitude journey, I did two more things to build my trust in the Lord: I made a timeline of spiritual waypoints and I made an Ebenezer. I drew a long, horizontal line down the center of the paper and jotted my different ages at the vertical lines. Once the framework was drawn, I remembered moments I felt God near, moments I knew He was real and moments of victory. Samples:

- Age 9-Became a believer at T Bar M Sports camp in New Braunfels, Texas.
- Age 10-Met my best friend, Alissa.

- Age 13-Experienced a miracle when God healed my knee.
- Age 23-Baptized at the farm.

As I wrote down each event, I felt my trust build. I saw the dots connect and I began to see the tracings of His fingertips.

We can trust God to show up in our lives. It may not be in the way or the time we expect, but He is always working. That's what we can trust—His heart for us.

I now take a posture of curiosity in life. We can be curious about what God is doing even when we are disappointed. We can trust that His love for us is steadfast. He will never quit you and me. *Can I get an amen?*

My Ebenezer is a milk jar piled high with rocks and sand. What seems like a quirky art project is actually one of the most meaningful objects I own. On each of those rocks, I've written why God is trustworthy and why I can put my hope in Him.

First Samuel 7 recounts the story of Samuel and includes the term *Ebenezer.* Samuel was a prophet, priest and judge in Israel. He led the nation of Israel to repent and fervently prayed for the Israelites. When God gave the Israelites victory over the Philistines, Samuel honored the Lord by building an altar to remember the victory. He called this altar *Ebenezer,* which meant "stone of help." It became a sign of victory, a marker of the Israelites' victory given by the grace and provision of the Lord.

My Ebenezer sits prominently on my nightstand. I found the milk jar at that same antique store in Littleton where I met Sherri. The bottom of the jar is filled with sand I gathered from the shore of my baptism at our family's farm. The thirty stones each have a memory or moment written on it (from the timeline I made) to remind me of God's victory and presence in my life.

One rock says, "Give Yourself Grace." Another rock says, "Oh, Lord Jesus Come," which was my plea on the day I got baptized. A third rock says, "Safety" and represents all the times God has protected me.

I trusted God only after tracing His fingertips and realizing He was good. Gratitude opened my way up to trust and trust allowed me to hope. That milk jar sits on my nightstand as a testament to all God has done.

God will never leave us or forsake us no matter how scared we may be. We just need to open our eyes and see.

Ebenezer

Instructions for how to make
your Ebenezer on page 103

QUESTIONS FOR THE MEANWHILE:

1. On a scale of 1-10 (10 being the most grateful), how grateful do you feel for your season in life right now?

2. Would you describe yourself as a contented or discontent person? What might need to change to become more content?

3. What kind of gratitude challenge do you need to take in your life?

4. How has your trust in the Lord increased or decreased based on the circumstances of life?

Counselor's Corner

Write Your Gifts of Gratitude

As I've shared my journey, let me challenge you to start counting. As you mentally snap photos and name gifts, you will find reasons to trust and to celebrate all God is doing. I hope you begin to feel joy in these moments of stillness.

Here's what you can do:
1. Purchase a journal and decide a place for it, perhaps your kitchen or bedroom. Set a pen beside it.
2. Carve out a few minutes each day to write 3-5 gifts for which you are thankful. They can be as small as the way soap glitters in the light or as large as a rekindled relationship.

Open your eyes. Our awareness of these gifts will grow over time.

3. After recording these gifts in your journal, take a picture of physical gifts or share your observations with a friend so that you can create a cemented memory of the blessing.

4. As you pay attention and pause to record, talk with and listen to God:

    a. What do you want me to do with these blessings you have brought into my life lately?

    b. What are You teaching me?

    c. What do you want me to do with these revelations?

    d. Thank you for healing and redeeming!

5. And when you forget His goodness, remember where He has shown up by turning back and re-reading your journal(s). His gifts of gratitude are moments to cherish.

How to Build Your Ebenezer:

1. Draw a timeline of spiritual waypoints in your life.

2. Purchase a jar from a local crafts or antique store.

3. Purchase a bag of rocks from a local crafts store or collect your own.

4. On each rock write a moment and/or memory that reminds you of a specific way that God has provided for you.

5. Put something meaningful, like sand or dirt from a specific place, at the base of your jar. Or simply pile the rocks inside.

6. Place the Ebenezer in your home as a memorial to what God has done so that you can remember to hope when fear, disappointment, or sadness creep in.

7. Let the jar become a conversation starter about God's goodness.

Chapter Twelve
Hope

"There are burning bushes everywhere."
~Ann Voskamp

My friend Erin has taught me a great deal about hope. At twenty-four-years-old, she married her high school sweetheart. However, after two years of a horribly painful marriage, she got a divorce. Erin packed up and moved to Denver to start over.

Lies defrauded her newlywed bliss. When I asked her what it was like she said, "Bewildering. My expectations got blown apart. I've never been a big planner, but I thought my life would generally follow the pattern. Graduate college, get married, buy a house, and start having kids. It's been a time of awakening, defining, and whittling life down to what's most important. It's been refining. I lost what I thought life was and learned what it really is: beautiful and terrible."

One morning over donuts and coffee, I asked her, "What did you think about God when your divorce happened? Was it hard to trust Him when things seemed to dissolve around you?"

"I learned a lot about God" she said, "That He's patient and good regardless of how uncomfortable life may become. He wants to make me more like Jesus. And that process is the most beautiful and painful thing imaginable. He's given me a task: to love Him and love others. That's my job in this life, and wherever I find myself along the way, that's what I'm supposed to keep doing."

Erin's experience could give her excuses to wallow in self-pity or harbor hatred, but she doesn't take them. Instead, Erin has chosen to trust in God despite her ex-husband's choices and her decision to get a divorce. She moved to Denver and started working and rebuilding. She believed the Lord could bring beauty from ashes. And so, she hoped.

"I don't care what else may happen in my life because I know God is there, and that's enough. I learned God will meet me in my darkest hour and that He knows what it feels like. He's with me. That's enough."

Erin said goodbye to the man she had said "I do" to. She packed up wedding gifts. She said goodbye to her home. All before she was 28. If I were Erin, I would've felt hopeless. I would've doubted God's goodness as I did in my story. Erin didn't. She knew God's character. She knew He was good and that more goodness could be found. Even when Erin found out the truth about her husband, Erin made a choice to hope. She took the empty void left by him and instead filled it with a dream. She had always wanted to move west. Now was her chance.

Erin adds, "I've learned that attitude makes all the difference. It's a good thing to learn from what goes on in life. Being angry and bitter is a waste of time and energy. Forgiveness is painful but it's much lighter. I'm not waiting around for anything either. I've chosen love and forgiveness.

"I realize this world is broken, but God loves me, He loves us. I don't know what's next and that's ok. We've been promised trouble in this life, but we've also been told to have hope that we'll see the goodness of the Lord in the land of the living. If you look for it, you'll surely see it. His goodness is in the sunset, the healed relationship, and also the hard times. It's the hard times that allow us to depend on Him, to be a helpless child again, hidden in the palm of a good Father. God offers us salvation and His constant presence here on this earth. The promise isn't: comfort, health, ease, happiness, or success. The promise is Him. We can always abide in *more* of Him. I've chosen to believe that and remove all other expectations. I have chosen to hope in the fact that God is near and that's freed me up to live my life with wonder and thankfulness."

I have never heard Erin complain. Really. She knows what she needs and if there's a morning she's fearful or sad, she spends extra time talking to the Father. She doesn't even re-hash it with us later. She's one of the most contented people I know. And I think it's because she knows God. She bathes in His peace.

On the one-year anniversary of her divorce, Erin invited six girls to dinner. I was coming late from work and walked in after everyone had been seated. They were at a table in the back facing the bay window that exposed the bright lights of the Denver skyline. I gave Erin a hug and sat down across from her in the open seat.

"How are you doing?" I asked. Erin smiled at me from across the table, "I'm actually doing okay. I don't feel angry anymore. I just pray for him. I spent a few hours journaling this morning and let the sadness come when it did. But I feel good and I feel free. And I'm so thankful to have all of you here with me. I mean, take a look around, a table full of girls I love and the city lights behind us, what more could I want?" It would have made complete sense for Erin to be self-consumed that evening. Instead, she went around the table and asked each of us about our days and how our weeks had been. I smiled as I watched her love and trust bravely.

I was honored to be at Erin's table that evening, and I felt even more grateful to glean from her. After our meal, the seven of us walked outside for a picture. We stood on the sidewalk with the skyline behind us, put our arms around one another and squeezed in tightly. Completely free and smiling big, Erin stood in the middle, in absolute love with God and others. The flash went off, and I smiled at my friend. She's still one of the bravest women I know.

We believe we know when, where and how God will deliver. But, how He shows up can surprise us. Think back to the moment Abraham was about to sacrifice Isaac because God had told him to. When Abraham picked up his knife and turned towards Isaac, an angel of the Lord stopped him. As Abraham looked up, he saw a ram caught by its horns in a nearby thicket. He took the ram and sacrificed it as a burnt offering instead of his son. That's the beauty of the ram. A lamb would have been expected for the traditional burnt offering Abraham prepared but God supplied a ram instead. If we don't open our eyes, we may miss the ram He is giving because we're too busy expecting the lamb.

God see you and He cares for you. He may bring you a sign when you need to be reminded He's near. He may bring you a friend when you least expect it. And He may restore the places long devastated (Isaiah 61:4). I returned to Denver for a winter wedding. It was Erin's. In God's goodness, Erin fell in love again. As I sat at the back of the church, tears filled my eyes. I smiled when I heard my brave friend trust, hope and say "I do."

QUESTIONS FOR THE MEANWHILE:

1. What are some signs or "burning bushes" God has given you to have greater hope along the way?

2. What have been some unexpected blessings the Lord has provided in your life? Thank Him for sending a ram when you expected the lamb.

3. Who in your life has taught you how to hope? What lessons did they teach you?

4. What friends has God provided in your life to help you stay the course with Him? Think about the friends at Erin's dinner. Who would sit at your table?

Scripture to Memorize:

"Be strong. Take courage. Don't be intimidated.
Don't give them a second thought because, God your
God is striding ahead of you. He's right there with
you. He won't let you down. He won't leave you"
(Deuteronomy 31:6, THE MESSAGE).

Chapter Thirteen
Waiting Gracefully

"Let not our longing slay the appetite of our living...
we accept and thank God for what is given, not
allowing the not-given to spoil it. This is the call.
This is the order of our lives. There is nothing
haphazard about them. We can commit to
God, and accept them from Him."
~Elisabeth Elliot - *Let me be a Woman*

Heather and Daniel had been married for three weeks when Daniel
was diagnosed with the most aggressive type of Leukemia. His
white blood count was at 63,000. A normal range is around 15,000.
Heather and Daniel were just twenty-three at the time.

I can hardly imagine. At twenty-three, I was not worried about
becoming a widow. Heather was.

The couple hadn't even gone on their honeymoon yet. In fact,
after years of waiting, they couldn't even kiss for six months after the
diagnosis.

When I met Heather, she and Daniel were near the end of
treatment. There had been three rounds of chemotherapy, 34 lumbar
punctures and a stem cell transplant. The couple was not new to cancer.
Family members had undergone battles over the years. And Heather was
a Leukemia nurse in the same hospital where Daniel would undergo
treatment and eventually recover.

The first time I met Heather, I was at a loss for words. I expected a woman fraught with tears and pleas. That kind of reaction would have made sense. But, Heather was peaceful. She sat across from me—calm, assured. She spoke confidently of the Lord's goodness and accepted her husband's diagnosis.

When I think of Heather, I think of Proverbs 31:25 (English Standard Version). "Strength and dignity are her clothing, and she laughs at the time to come." Fyodor Dostoevsky once said, "There is only one thing that I dread: not to be worthy of my sufferings." I want to be a woman worthy of my waiting. Heather taught me how to do that.

Heather is a woman who waits gracefully when so often, I have waited selfishly. She never asks "what about me?" Instead, she serves her husband. Heather spoke of the fear she had when she and Daniel first went home from the hospital. She had nightmares that his cancer had come back. She feared falling asleep because then, who would watch Daniel? What if she woke up and found him dead?

Heather feared being enough for Daniel. All she could do was let him rest. That was it. Imagine the nights of waiting, sleeping in a hospital room beside your twenty-three-year-old groom. Wondering, will healing come?

Viktor Frankl was a Holocaust survivor who wrote the book, *Man's Search for Meaning*. Frankl says the men who were worthy of their suffering were the ones who turned their pain into an inner achievement—a spiritual freedom. Our ability to respond to the circumstances of life is the one freedom we'll never lose.

Frankl says, "Those who have a 'why' to live, can bear with almost any 'how.'" Heather found peace in her suffering by finding a "why". She and Daniel viewed his diagnosis as an opportunity to better trust and fear the Lord. They had faith that God knew better than they did. He was going to work out everything according to His plan.

Through her waiting, Heather remained brave, dignified and unselfish. She made use of her waiting by abiding deep in the Father. It was He who gave her an unbreakable strength. That is a woman worthy of waiting.

Viktor Frankl says, "Suffering is similar to the behavior of gas. If a certain quantity of gas is pumped into an empty chamber, it will fill the chamber completely and evenly, no matter how big the chamber. Thus suffering completely fills the human soul and conscious mind, no matter whether the suffering is great or little. Therefore the "size" of human suffering is absolutely relative."

I'm going to go ahead and make an assumption about you. If you are reading this, I suspect you're waiting for something. Whatever you are waiting for, I want you to know it is okay to have a feeling about it. There is no judgment for *why* you are hurting. It's the *how* that makes a difference. There's the family member that doesn't know Jesus. The dream that is broken. The grieving that never ends. The child you're hoping to conceive. It's agonizing to wait.

I do not want to sound trite and I do not want to diminish your longing, so hear me say this: unfulfilled desire can be heart wrenching and it stings in places we never knew existed. God sees you and He hears you. I promise.

You are not forgotten, even if it feels like it. Hang in there. God's compassion for you is warm and it is tender.

Heather was found in the hospital waiting room. Maybe you're waiting on your knees—begging God to give you the desires of your heart. This is my question for all of us—"are we waiting gracefully or are we waiting selfishly?"

I don't want to waste the waiting. I want to use my longings to add a deeper meaning to my life. I want my perceived lacking to push me into a deeper relationship with the Lord. Elisabeth Elliot says, "Let not our longing slay the appetite of our living." Am I missing my life because I'm too busy longing? Let's not get so distracted by the instability of the *Meanwhile* that we miss out on the ministry of it.

As a counselor, I'm in the business of telling people they can feel really hard and scary things. Certain emotions are more uncomfortable to experience but emotions are fleeting. There is comfort in knowing that although every emotion has an intensity cycle, and you might be at the top of it, emotions typically last up to twenty minutes.

John Piper says, "My feelings are not God. God is God." It is best if we view emotions as tools, not as truth. We can submit our emotions to God and ask Him to guide us. Ask yourself, "I am feeling___so what do I need? I am feeling ___so what does God want me to do about it?" I am feeling ___, where is God in this?

Emotions can reveal all kinds of things. We might have peace if we're headed in the right direction or angst if we're not. Emotions can reveal what we need from God (see the table of God's attributes at the end of chapter seven) just as emotions can prompt us to confess, to celebrate or to change directions in our life.

I best identify and experience emotions by journaling. I know Heather does too. At the end of this chapter is an Expressive Writing Exercise as well as a table of feelings. I'd encourage you to use these worksheets when you feel stuck in a feeling. As you write, envision pouring your soul out to God. Be as honest as you can be.

Prayer is intimacy with God. It is not a wish list for Santa-god to fill. God has compassion on us as we ask "why," "when," and for "how long." But eventually, to move to a place of believing, we'll have to start asking "what now?" What do we do now God? We need to focus on "what is" instead of "what if." Write and pray until you know what to do. For help on turning your emotions into prayer, use "Taking my Emotions to God" at the end of this chapter.

We might want to hide from God when we're hurting. We tend to control with clenched hands. But, we don't have to have it all together. That is far from biblical. Do what you need to do to become dependent on the Lord. Wrestle. Crawl. Flail. Limp. He'll give you more grace. I promise.

I know how stuck one can feel when waiting. But, there's hope. All seasons will come to an end. There are seasons of dancing and there are seasons of crying. There are times to heal and there are times to build. You might be feeling stuck right now but hang on, a new season will come. That's the beauty of a season. It's temporary.

Heather waited gracefully by waiting graciously. She captivated her thoughts (2 Corinthians 10:4) and wrote it in concrete: God is good no matter what. Period. When we find ourselves longing, let's remember the Truth:

- God is for you.
- God will take care of you.
- God sees you.
- God claims you.
- God will answer you.
- God will never leave you.
- God will always love you.
- God will keep you safe.
- God will work out all things according to His purposes (if we allow it.)

My favorite counseling technique is called reframing. Reframing is the active process of seeing something differently. It's how we learn to see experiences through a lens of hope and truth. Heather constantly reframed. She chose to wait gracefully by waiting graciously. Heather accepted and thanked God for what was given while turning over what was taken. She thanked the Lord for her experience as a Leukemia nurse. She was glad the couple's apartment was already close to the hospital. She relished in the love of friends and family. And she was grateful she and Daniel had extra time together after remission. A gift most couples can't enjoy until retirement.

We can reframe any experience in life. Here are several examples of how we can reframe.

1. I can't do anything right. Reframe: What was the last successful thing you did?

2. I'm scared. Reframe: If instead you felt fearless, what would you be doing?

3. I hate the job I'm in. Reframe: What kind of opportunities do you have in your job that you might not have elsewhere?

4. I don't have any weekend plans. I wonder why people don't include me? Reframe: Perhaps this is a chance for you to invite

a new friend to do something with you. With a weekend completely open to yourself, what are some chores you could get caught up on or what are some fun, new spots around town you could explore?

Galatians 6:9 says, "Let us not become weary in doing good, for at the proper time we will reap a harvest if we do not give up." What kind of harvest are we reaping while we wait? We can't choose every circumstance or delay in our life but we always get to choose our response.

Every situation, good or bad, is an opportunity. It is an opportunity to believe and act upon the Truth, not the lie—God is good no matter what. That's how we can honor Him. By believing Him. God does not delay. He is always on the move. When life seems at a standstill, He is either protecting us or preparing us. If we let Him, He will do something beautiful in the in-between.

Heather created deeper meaning to her life through Daniel's diagnosis. Her faith was strengthened, her foundation made secure. How Heather waited revealed what she believed about God. Daniel is now in full remission. The couple has moved to a new city and is enjoying a second chance at being newlyweds. I learned how to suffer well from Heather. God provided a miracle the day he healed Daniel. But, here's the truth. Even if He hadn't, Heather would have still called Him good in her grief. That is a woman and that is a God worthy of praise.

QUESTIONS FOR THE MEANWHILE:

1. What did you learn from Heather and Daniel's story?

2. How has suffering been used to create deeper meaning in your life?

3. In what ways are you waiting gracefully? In what ways are you waiting selfishly?

4. What is one way to wait graciously this week?

5. Look back on your life. What divine delays have occurred for your protection and/or preparation?

6. What do you need to reframe in your life today?

7. Based on the way you wait, what is this saying about your belief in God?

Counselor's Corner

How to Wait Gracefully

Use the following exercises to help you wait. If you are stuck on a feeling, look at the feelings table to help you discern what you are feeling. You can then process your emotions by using the expressive writing exercise before turning your feelings and writings into a prayer or using Scripture to do so.

Feelings Table

Sad	Glad	Mad	Scared
Blue	Happy	Angry	Fearful
Depressed	Ecstatic	Bitter	Anxious
Lonely	Excited	Resentful	Frightened
Confused	Peaceful	Upset	Overwhelmed
Lost	Mellow	Agitated	Uneasy
Disappointed	Relieved	Touchy	Insecure
Hurt	Satisfied	Frustrated	Worried

Expressive Writing Exercise Instructions

At least three times a week, write down your deepest thoughts and feelings about your current situation in life. Try to allow one day between each exercise and consider setting a consistent time and place for each submission such as Mondays / Wednesdays / Fridays or Tuesdays / Thursdays / Saturdays. Please use your Expressive Writing Log to record the number of times you write each week, the theme of what you write about and the duration for which you write.

In your writing, record both positive and negative feelings. Do not worry about grammar, spelling, sentence structure, or handwriting. Focus instead on the content and pouring out your soul.

Expressive Writing Exercise Log

	MON	TUES	WED	THU	FRI	SAT	SUN
WHEN							
DURA-TION							
THEMES							

	MON	TUES	WED	THU	FRI	SAT	SUN
WHEN							
DURA-TION							
THEMES							

	MON	TUES	WED	THU	FRI	SAT	SUN
WHEN							
DURA-TION							
THEMES							

Waiting Gracefully-Prayer Exercise

1. POUR OUT YOUR SOUL: Acknowledge your emotions. Ask the Holy Spirit to help you identify what emotions you are feeling. Use the chart above if you get stuck.

2. WRESTLE: Write to God what you feel and why.

3. LET IT GO: What are your emotions telling you? What thoughts are true, what thoughts are untrue?

4. TRUST AND HAVE FAITH: Choose to agree with God's Word and God's character. Then choose to act on that truth, relying on the Holy Spirit to empower you.

Waiting Gracefully-Pray Through Scripture

There are several ways to pray through the Scriptures. We can do so verbatim. We can meld together different verses to pray through them. We can use our names in the passages. Or, we can re-write or paraphrase the Scriptures. Below are two Psalms to re-write in your words. Clients have found deep healing in doing this.

1. Rewrite Psalm 13 (NIV) in your words.

How long, O Lord? Will you forget me forever?
How long will you hide your face from me?
(Example: God, where are you? How long will you ignore me?)

How long must I take counsel in my soul
and have sorrow in my heart all the day?
How long shall my enemy be exalted over me?

Consider and answer me, O Lord my God;
light up my eyes, lest I sleep the sleep of death,

lest my enemy say, "I have prevailed over him,"
lest my foes rejoice because I am shaken.

But I have trusted in your steadfast love;
my heart shall rejoice in your salvation.

I will sing to the Lord, because he has dealt bountifully with me.

2. Rewrite Psalm 23 (NIV) in your words.

The Lord is my shepherd; I shall not want.
(Example: The Lord will take care of me. He will meet every need.)

He makes me lie down in green pastures.
He leads me beside still waters.[a]

He restores my soul.
He leads me in paths of righteousness
for his name's sake.

Even though I walk through the valley of the shadow of death,[c]
I will fear no evil, for you are with me;

your rod and your staff,
they comfort me.

You prepare a table before me
in the presence of my enemies;
you anoint my head with oil;
 my cup overflows.

Surely goodness and mercy shall follow me
all the days of my life,
and I shall dwell in the house of the Lord forever.

Chapter Fourteen
Purpose

"The antidote to exhaustion may not be rest but
wholeheartedness... we are typically exhausted because
we are not doing our TRUE work."
~Gordon T. Smith - *Courage and Calling*

Identity exploration is part of growing up. We try on new careers,
new friends, new tattoos, and new relationships as we try to figure
out who we are and why God put us on this earth. We want to find
meaning and significance when so many things feel unknown. Millennials want to be seen and known, and we want to find our place on
this crazy orb of land and sea. Millennials are more than just a cultural
statistic. In their book, *TwentySomeone,* Craig Dunham and Doug Ser-
ven define millennials as Twenty-Somebodies with unique identities
and purposes.

I made counseling my identity, my reason for being put on this
earth, but I fell short of realizing my actual purpose. I placed significance
on the therapist's chair but was unaware to the responsibility it carried
with it until I started seminary. According to Kottler in *On Being a
Therapist,* "The therapist strongly desires to rescue clients because there
is so much at stake for her own self-worth." I saw my value in being
able to see and hear people. I always had. I assumed people loved me
because of my effort to love them back and to do it well.

This began when I was in the third grade. My class was outside
playing, and as I walked to the monkey bars, I noticed a girl sitting
alone at the base of a tall tree, the one we played hide-and-seek around.

She got picked on a lot in school. Something in my tiny heart led me in her direction. I asked if she wanted to play with me on the monkey bars, and a smile stretched across her freckle-laden cheeks. It felt good to include her. It felt like God wanted me to.

Tim Keller explains in his book, *Counterfeit Gods*, that when something in our lives becomes essential for our self-worth and our happiness, that thing is an idol. Counseling became my idol when I moved to Colorado. I clung to it for validation and I wanted to play the savior.

Keller goes on to say that when these idols are threatened, we become absolute in our anger. "If we don't confront the very idol we are enchained to, we'll never be able to master our anger." When counseling didn't feel like a good fit, I became inconsolable. My self-worth was being rattled. But, it needed to be.

I spent a lot of time on planes between Texas and Denver during my first year of seminary. I carried textbooks with me to stay on top of my reading. On one flight back to Texas I began to read my Psychopathology textbook. Psychopathology is the study of mental disorders. The Greek origins of the word psychopathology can be boiled down to the study of the suffering soul. I love learning about the suffering soul. I felt a surge of pride every time I told someone I was studying to become a counselor. I felt important. And yet it became more about my expertise than the suffering soul.

As I read my textbook on the plane, the woman next to me looked over my shoulder and asked what I was studying. I told her I hoped to become a counselor one day. The woman leaned in closer so that only she and I could hear her words. "My son had a suicide attempt last year," she said. "He still hasn't been able to recover. I'm not sure what I'm supposed to do. What have they told you to do in school?" Gulp.

She looked at me like I could save her son, like I could somehow free his soul from whatever was plaguing it. She needed me, and she didn't even know me. But I wasn't a superhero with magical powers. I didn't own anything close to a cape. I told her, "I'm so sorry to hear about your son." Looking back, I wish I had asked her something: a question to engage her and encourage her to speak about her son.

A professor told us we should never work harder than our clients. The issue with finding identity in what we do for a living is that we will always work harder than our clients—whoever those clients may be.

That's not only exhausting but it's also an unstable way of living. That's one of the reasons I quit practicum for a period of time. I placed so much importance on my client's recovery that I linked it to my worth. Misplaced identities have to be torn down like any other idol.

Vocation

Gordon T. Smith says that there is a stark difference between vocation and career. According to Smith, our vocations are God-given. Vocation, like purpose, is a reflection of our fundamental identity; it is our reason for being. Vocations are transferable across time, space and career choice. Whether we quit, get fired or retire, our vocation will remain. Vocation (purpose) is how we live out our identity. This identity is the essence of who we are.

Identity is what we have left if everything—jobs, accolades, relationships—is stripped away. Identity is what I have left even if I a client never recovers.

Smith says Christians have three specific vocations to live out in this life:

1. First, we are called to love God and to love others.
2. Second, we are to discern how we are uniquely called to do this.
3. Third, we are called to take care of the daily tasks and responsibilities we have been given.

There will always be bills to pay, laundry to fold and groceries to buy. We can live out our vocation in our career choice as well as in other ways.

I am not a full-time counselor because I took a job that allowed me health benefits. I chose a career in counseling because it best allows me to live out my identity and purpose. As a person, my personality aligns with that of a counselor. As a vocation, counseling allows me to love God and love others by seeing and hearing people so that they might feel cared for.

My vocation means I'm also responsible to be a loving sister, a gracious friend and a steady renter who pays on time. It's simply irresponsible to cast off budgets and responsibilities for the sake of our vocations.

Find Your Vocation

I used to like thinking people thought I knew the deep, hidden secret to human suffering and healing. But I don't. It's not me doing the healing. It's the real Counselor, the Holy Spirit, who heals the people I work with. I'm just the body in the seat.

God allows me to live out my vocation in my career. Even though this is the case, there are still unfulfilling days. If our purpose is tied up in what we feel or in what we do and don't do, we'll burn out. It's called compassion fatigue. The weeks I'm most tired are the weeks I realize my vocation got lost.

When a career is lived in the right direction, it gives life. When a career is used to give us an identity, we steal life from others and ourselves. Counseling must be the vehicle I use to live out my vocation to see and to hear, not the other way around.

I started my search for identity and purpose at the wrong end of things. I looked to counseling for validation and purpose when I should have looked to God for those. I had to separate the two, and a Career Development course helped me do so.

While in class, we read *Courage and Calling* by Gordon T. Smith to help us discern our purpose and recognize how vocation and identity interact. He lays out the following steps to finding our God-given vocation:

1. Know Yourself
   - "Who am I?"
   - "What makes me unique?"
   - "How has God called me?"
   - "What are my gifts and abilities?"

- "What is the deepest desire of my heart?"
- "What is my unique personality and temperament?"

2. Identify Your Gifts and Abilities
   - "What are your "nonstrengths" and strengths?"

3. What is Your Deepest Desire?
   - "What do you long for?"
   - "What brings you the greatest joy?"
   - "When you are right with God and put aside your desire for wealth, comfort, security and acceptance, what remains?"

4. How Do You Recognize the World's Need?
   - "Where do you see the brokenness of the world?"

5. What is Your Unique Personality or Temperament?
   - "Are you an extrovert or introvert?"
   - "How do you process information? Do you think in terms of possibilities as an intuitive or do you rely more on clear and concrete facts as a sensate?"
   - "Do you make decisions as a thinker or as a feeler? Thinkers rely on logic while feelers rely on the personal implications of a choice."
   - "Do you prefer spontaneity or closure? A perceiver appreciates the process leading up to a decision whereas a judger finds greater fulfillment after a decision is made."

6. What Does Community Reveal About Your Self?
   - "Become aware of how your gifts and abilities contribute to the community you are in."
   - "In what ways are you different or similar to those in your community?"

Know Your Self

The perfect time to find your vocation is now. Learning who we are can feel like a gift or a burden. But the gift is greater. My time in Colorado was the breeding ground for this search. I used many tools to discern my vocation. First, I met with my mentor Melonie. Second, I took personality assessments (the Ennegram, Self-Directed Search, The Strong Instrument, DISC Test, Strengths Finder and the Myers-Briggs) and walked through the discoveries I found from those tests. Third, I walked through the steps that Smith laid out above.

Another professor explained that to find your purpose, you must assess the lens through which you see the world. When I look at the world around me, I see people. No matter where I go or what I do, I see people.

I know no greater honor than when people unveil the wounds deep within and allow me to touch them. God used my decision to give up counseling to take away the idol of it. What I was once enchained to, I am now free of. I had to give it up in order to learn my true vocation. My vocation isn't to counsel, it is to connect to people by seeing and hearing them.

Choose a Career

Not every job we take will feed our greatest passion. Sometimes, we need to take a job to make ends meet, to support our family or to have work-life balance. That's why vocation is important. If I were a receptionist, a teacher or an accountant, I could still live out my purpose of connecting with people.

There is insurmountable pressure these days to choose the right career. Many of us ended up in a career that has nothing to do with our major. I was a Marketing major, because a business degree made good logical sense and I wanted to own my private practice one day. I got an English minor because writing was my first love, and I needed to write some poetry along the way.

I chose a career based on my vocation, my responsibilities and my short-term and long-term goals. As I searched for that first job out of seminary I made a list of pros and cons and I thought through what I wanted in life.

Based on the above, I chose a church job that has proven to be the perfect fit for this time in my life. I work in a faith-filled and encouraging environment. I have enough flexibility to plan new events for our women's ministry and work different hours each week to accommodate my client schedule.

There will be no perfect job, just like there is no perfect spouse, house or family. Every job will have parts of it we don't enjoy. For instance, some of my greatest work frustrations have come at the unclogging of the paper shredder or the reprinting of nametags that have taken me six times to print correctly. God calls us to serve and to walk humbly (Micah 6:8). I know no greater place to practice this than in the workplace.

My parents beautifully model marketplace ministry. Before meetings, my dad leads his staff in prayer. There are Bible studies held in the conference room. And on a weekly basis, two chaplains come through the office to meet and pray with employees. The ministry that happens at that office is equal to the ministry done in the church. That's what's beautiful about having a job in corporate America. You are able to love and reach people in a distinctly different way from the church. God is just as real and alive in the cubicle as He is in the chapel.

Find a place to work where someone wants to invest in you, personally and professionally. Align your vocation with your career role, but remember that a job is far too small to hold your identity and all of your gifts, interests and talents. Be responsible and look at the salary and number of hours you'll have to work. Choose a career that lines up with your lifestyle and where there is a void in vocation or in interest, seek chances to volunteer or begin a new hobby. And don't let ego get in the way. We all have to start somewhere and though it doesn't feel like it, we are still young with a lot to learn.

Bill Hybels says, "Simplified living is about more than doing less. It's being who God called us to be, with a wholehearted, single-minded focus. It's walking away from innumerable lesser opportunities in favor of the few to which we've been called and for which we've been created. Our vocation is congruent with how God made us. Do it. Be true to who you are. Be true to your call, true to how God made you."

Take the time in your twenties and thirties to discover how God made you uniquely you. Find a mentor, find a counselor, and answer the questions above or take a personality assessment.

The Lord our God is a creative Father. He has fashioned you in a particular way. Who does God say you are? Take that identity and transfer it to how you live. All of us love God and love people in different ways. Figure out how you best do this, and do it.

QUESTIONS FOR THE MEANWHILE:

1. Answer the questions from *Courage and Calling* listed above.

2. What is your career and what is your vocation? How are they similar, and how are they different?

3. As you navigate the *Meanwhile*, what have you learned about your identity and purpose?

4. What hobbies or volunteer activities would help you share your purpose and passion?

Counselor's Corner

Take Career Counseling Assessments

For resources in discerning your purpose and getting help with a career decision, visit ncda.org (National Career Development Association) and search for a professional in your area to help you make career decisions.

To take one of the assessments previously mentioned in this chapter, you can find these resources at:
1. Ennegram: A personality test understood as a typology of nine different personality types.
2. Ennegraminstitute.com
3. DISC: A behavior assessment tool based on four different personality types.

4. Discprofile.com

5. Strengths Finder: A tool that assesses your natural talents and ranks your strengths.

6. Strengthsfinder.com

7. Myers-Briggs: Measures individual preferences by personality type. There are 16 possible combinations.

8. Myersbriggs.org

9. Self-Directed Search (SDS): Self-administered and self-scored. The test provides a summary code that represents one's personality type and environmental model including: realistic, investigative, artistic, social, enterprising and conventional.

10. Self-directed-search.com

11. The Strong Instrument: This test helps with choosing a college major, exploring career options, career development, employee engagement and career reintegration.

12. Cpp.com

Choosing a Career

There are many different reasons we choose a career. In addition to the questions listed in this chapter, here are several more to help you discern what career to pursue:

1. My dad says everyone has a "PEG" (passion, experience and gifts). Our purpose is our "PEG." What are you passionate about? What unique experiences have you had growing up? What are your spiritual gifts? What other gifts do you have?

2. Growing up, what value did your family place on work?

3. What did you dad do for a living? Your mom?

4. What did you want to be when you were younger?

5. What was your favorite class growing up?

6. What have you liked and disliked about every job you've had?

7. What extracurricular activities did you enjoy over the years and what roles or leadership positions did you enjoy? What characteristics did you need for these roles?

8. Think about the encouragement you've received from others over the years. What have people told you that you excel in?

9. If you were on a sports team or team of any kind, what role did you play? Were you the MVP, the team captain, the one who cheered everyone on, the first to the gym?

10. What have you learned you *don't* want to do for a living?

11. What people groups has God called you to love?

12. Who do you need to provide for in your career? A spouse? Family member? Children? Just yourself?

13. What kind of work/life balance would you prefer? Are you willing to work late nights and/or weekends?

14. Is there a non-traditional avenue of work you'd like to pursue? Perhaps a hybrid of several different types of jobs?

15. Name one way to be healthy. One way to express creativity. And one way to give. Often times, where we can't live out our passion in work, we can place it in one of these categories.

Chapter Fifteen
Giving

"Nothing you have not given away
will ever really be yours."
~C.S. Lewis

I currently live across the street from an assisted living care center. Every night, when I close my blinds, I notice one window. The light is on late into the evening, and the drapes are pulled to one side. When I crawl into bed, I wonder who might live there. I wonder if that sweet man or woman has family or friends who visit them. I wonder why they are up so late and how they pass the time. I like to peer out my window at the passersby walking to the neighborhood restaurant below my window, and I think, maybe the man or woman in the window likes to watch them too. I want to know who lives behind that window. But I haven't met them yet, because I have been selfish with my time.

Millennials are known for being self-focused. But these years can instead become a time of giving. We have the freedom and time to give. I made a list of everything I want to accomplish before the next phase of my life. But when I took a second look, there was not one goal that had anything to do with serving or loving others.

The church where I work hosted a class about how older adults can communicate with Millennials. At the beginning of the class, the pastor I was assisting posed the question, "At what point does a Millennial become an adult?" Surely the answer couldn't be having a house, six-figure salary, spouse or babies. I scanned the room and saw one of our most respected church members raise his hand. "I believe someone becomes an adult when they learn to look outside of one's self to serve others and become able to prioritize others' needs above their own." Now that's something God can help me do.

Growing up I felt I was as selfless as any kid could be. When I became a twenty-something, though, something changed. I constantly thought, *What about me? Who's going to take care of me?* I didn't realize it then, but this was fertile ground for Satan to move in. I became consumed with myself—my emotions, needs, wants, thoughts and desires.

On one visit home, my mom called me selfish. She had really good reason to, but I had never been called that before. It was a wake-up call. I can't exist for myself only. I needed to learn how to choose better by serving others. I needed to move from being a consumer to a giver.

When I realized my mom was telling the truth, I emailed the youth director at the church I attended in Denver. I loved working with teenage girls, and I figured that'd be a good way to serve. I spent many afternoons and evenings on walks or splitting dinner with a younger girl.

At first, it was really difficult to forget about myself, but with time and conscious effort, my heart began to change. I hoped to give these girls what Melonie had given to me—a safe place to go.

God taught me something else during that time: we each help the other. While listening to one of my girls talk about all of the reasons she loved God I marveled at how free she looked as she spoke. I thought I was doing her a favor by taking her to lunch but God was also using her in my life.

We get to decide what we are going to be about. We can live for ourselves and find ourselves empty. Or, we can live for others and find fullness. On Valentine's Day eve I hosted a dinner for some girls. We indulged in homemade pasta and fudge brownies right out of the oven. I woke on Valentine's Day thinking of my mentor, Melonie, and how she and her husband deserved a date night. I chose to spend Valentine's with their two kids so that their parents could have the night out.

That evening was filled with pepperoni pizza on paper plates, spilled Dr. Pepper, and leftover candy from the kids' school parties that week. We played video games and watched a movie before I tucked the two of them into bed. As I shut off the lights to both of their bedrooms and walked back down the stairs, I thanked God. Melonie had given me so much of her patience, heart and time. It was right to pay it forward by watching her kids that night. Sometimes the best thing we can do with our time is to give it away.

Choose Better

We have each been given a specific vocation, transferrable skills, values, personality, interests and spiritual gifts. Vocation is often too large to fit into a single career, which is why it helps to align our vocation with volunteerism, hobbies, and worthwhile ventures.

God doesn't necessarily call us to volunteer with one specific organization over another, but I do believe He calls us to show His love no matter where we are. Delivering hand-written notes to encourage someone is a small thing, but it's one way to be selfless.

Find the involvement outside of work that best fits you. Shift the focus to finding your vocation. People around you need your time, energy, talents, and hearts. Write a note to the co-worker who looked down yesterday, make dinner for someone who is about to have a new baby, babysit for a couple who needs time alone, or offer to help a friend move.

I have seen friends who work as financial planners and lawyers volunteer their time by helping others prepare tax returns or understand legal documents. Think of what you do for a career and realize that there are plenty of others who do not have the same skills or experience as you do. How can you adapt these skills and expertise into a giving role? For instance, our Vacation Bible School is made all the better by the teachers who donate their time, heart and talents to teach our students.

We have the availability to give our time away, to choose better. How are we going to share our vocation with the world around us? What can we do with our skills and talents that might bring life to someone else?

God never called us to self-consumption. He called us to daily give our lives away. The best way we can do that is by using our vocation and the tools He gave us to see, hear and love those around us. Learn to live a life of giving, of others-centeredness.

QUESTIONS FOR THE MEANWHILE:

1. How do you currently share your time between family, work, recreation, and volunteering?

2. When would you describe yourself as a consumer? When would you describe yourself as a giver?

3. How have you moved past self-focus to truly focus on others? At what point does focusing on others become a selfish pursuit? How will you let God make you truly others-centered?

4. How do you spend your time? What are you doing? What are you thinking?

5. Name three specific ways you can donate your skills and expertise. Name both large and small actions (e.g.: Cutting out paper shapes for the Sunday School classes at church, taking youth on a mission trip, tutoring, teaching music/ acting or dance lessons, etc.)

Chapter Sixteen
Becoming

"There is a season for wildness and a season for
settledness, and this is neither. This season is about
becoming. Don't lose yourself at happy hour, but don't
lose yourself on the corporate ladder, either."
~Shauna Niequist

One Saturday I sat in a workshop for a counseling internship.
I would be interning at a faith-based crisis pregnancy center
and this was the first part of our training. Before we began flipping
through our binders, our instructor placed a stack of postcards on
the front table.

"Everyone take a postcard that represents where you are today.
After you pick one we'll introduce ourselves." I chose a postcard with
a little girl holding onto the string of a huge, red balloon. She stood
in a green field and everything about the picture was hopeful and
cheery.

When it was my turn, I stood to say, "My name's Amanda Grace
Caldwell and I'll be one of the interns this year at Alternatives. I
chose this picture because it looks like hope is lifting and that's how I
feel right now. This is my second chance to sit with clients and really
see them and hear them. I was scared to start over because the first time
I tried to be a counselor, I ended up quitting. But this is my redemption
round, and I feel like it's going to be okay this time."

I thought I had it all figured out post-college. I focused so much on arriving that I lost sight of becoming the person God made me to be. I questioned my clinical director's advice when she told me to settle down and enjoy the ride because I thought I knew better. I thought life was more about achieving than it was growing. Turns out, she was right.

I was no longer worried about being the best counselor. I was solely focused on loving as deeply and as effectively as I could. I had the privilege of standing in ultrasound rooms as women saw their babies for the first time. I heard stories of women who gave up everything to save a life. I treaded on holy ground as I watched years of shame break off of women in our post-abortion support group.

There were moments I knew what to say and moments I sat silent. There were long days and mistakes. But I was always learning. I gleaned from my clients who taught me about hope and bravery and the importance of family.

I was humbled at the persistence I saw in the woman who took four buses to get to our clinic and another who walked six miles just for an appointment. I would have missed out on all of those faces and all of those stories had I stayed stuck on myself.

The sacred space of those clinic rooms was always about becoming. It was in the mess and the chaos and the questions that a heartbeat was found. It was through the wrestling and the conversations that liberty happened. I'm so tired of living for the perfectly wrapped package tied up in a bow. What about that is biblical anyways? It's time for us to shift our focus to become.

Every semester I saw clients, I had to create a Professional Development Plan. The purpose of this was to process, with our mentor, a key area of our character we wanted to address. One of the goal statements I made was: "I want to become a person who has the courage to name and claim the values that make me who I am."

We listed growth markers to track how we changed internally and externally. We created learning strategies to help us become. These learning strategies included "Knowledge Strategies" and "Practice Strategies."

The knowledge strategies focused on resources used to gain knowledge about our chosen character area like in a book or an interview.

The practice strategies were observable activities we could engage in to help forge new patterns in the character area we described. A practice strategy I used with my goal statement was making a list of all of the values I had inherited from others (directly or indirectly) and sifting through them all until I came up with the list of values I wanted to own for myself. A few of the values I chose included kindness, hospitality, honesty and comfort.

Each plan has helped me become. I recommend you also make and evaluate a development plan. Don't get stuck in your season of waiting. Instead, shift your focus to becoming. Only then, can we best love God and serve those around us.

Shauna Niequist says our twenties and thirties are the perfect time to start asking ourselves some good questions:

- "Are we proud of the life we're living?"
- "Are we proud of the man or woman we are becoming?"

Niequist says there are those who used their 20s to learn and grow and become real live adults. On the other hand, there are those who meant to grow up, to stop living life like one big frat party. But they didn't. They didn't become. Instead, they're trapped in extended adolescence.

It matters who you spend time with. First Corinthians 15:33 says "Do not be misled: 'Bad company corrupts good character.'" (NIV). I am one-hundred percent all about outreach but I am also one-hundred percent all about spending time with people "better" than me. All the stories I tell in this book are about people better than me. Whether in boldness, freedom, fun, or calm, I have something to learn from all of them. We need people better than us to become. Now hear me out. I'm not encouraging comparison but I am encouraging discernment. Spend time with the gentle and patient. Learn from the joyful and loving. Take notes from the kind and self-controlled.

It matters what tribe we're a part of. We need to be encouraged and edified by those on the same path as us. We can't do this alone. I joined a small group in Houston and God built deep, life-giving relationships between the seven of us. All seven of us are different but we're also the same. Despite our different backgrounds or opinions, we all yearn to best live our lives for the Lord. And in that space, we encourage one another, we push one another and we love one another.

That has been my favorite thing about our group. We have truly chosen to support one another. As women in the same stage of life we're navigating similar courses and asking similar questions. I've never met another bunch of ladies so willing to celebrate. As a group, we celebrate anything (and each other). There are Sunday suppers, beach trips, birthday parties, words spoken over one another, flowers delivered to workplaces, gift cards, the list goes on.

As a group, we've navigated everything: family issues, new jobs, promotions, career difficulties, roommates, break-ups, falling in love. We did it all together. These women have helped me become. They have taught me what a woman of the Lord looks like and they have encouraged me to serve. There are those who give more than spend out of their paychecks and there are those who volunteer every chance they get.

Goal setting is an essential part of becoming. Researchers have found that you are 42% more likely to obtain your goals if you write them down. As we goal-set, it's important to remember the acronym SMART. Make goals that are specific, measurable, attainable, realistic and time-bound. A few goals on my sister Lindsey's list include turning her phone off at meals to better love who she's with, attending the Grammy's (which she did!), running a half-marathon and visiting the set of Shark Tank.

Three goals I wrote down include reading the Bible cover-to-cover, reading a new book every month and hosting a monthly Supper Club to encourage and love the women in my life through hospitality.

Mark Batterson in his book, *Circle Maker,* encourages readers to use categories when creating goals. Lindsey and I have taken Batterson's advice and made goals according to the following categories: Health, Financial, Educational, Relational, Spiritual, and Experiential.

Grab some colored pens and paper and spend some time with the Lord. Allow yourself the space to dream and to think. Are you proud of the woman (or man) you are becoming? Are you headed in the right direction? Write out the list of values you ascribe to. Are you living these out now? Make yourself a personal mission statement. It's easier to make a goal list if we know where we're going. We can't control everything but we can choose our trajectory. The exercises at the end of this chapter are lengthy (and weighty). Take the time to sit down and sift through it. I promise there is fruit there. Plan to become.

QUESTIONS FOR THE MEANWHILE:

1. What advice do you have for navigating the twenties and thirties well?

2. Who is part of your tribe?

3. What is one area of your character you would like to work on? What is the first step in growing in this area?

Counselor's Corner

Deliberately Become

1. Professional Development Plan
    a. Spend some time in prayer and ask God to show you the kind of person He wants you to become in this season. What area of your character does He want to grow? What has helped you recognize this as an area of growth?

    b. How will growth in this area impact the lives of others?

    c. Complete this goal statement: "I want to become a person who_____
    _____."

    d. Describe three specific growth markers that will indicate this change in your life.

    e. Write down two knowledge strategies. What resources can help your understanding of this area?

f. Write down four observable practice strategies. How can you practice this new growth area?

g. As you complete your strategies, set a deadline and frequency for each.

h. With whom will you process your journey?

i. Set an end date (aim for four months or more) and get started!

2. Goal List Worksheet
    a. Grab some sheets of paper and put aside one sheet per the following categories: current season in life (e.g. single, married, married with children, etc.) one-year goals, five-year goals and lifelong goals.

    b. Create your goals using the following categories (Health, Financial, Educational, Relational, Spiritual, and Experiential) or create your own.

    c. Think about your vocation and personal mission statement. What goals fit within these realms? Begin to write goals down in each of your four categories.

    d. Keep each goal SMART and specify an end date for each.

    e. Hang your goals where they are easy to see and check-off.

Chapter Seventeen
Decision-Making

"Learning to choose is hard. Learning to
choose well is harder. And learning to choose
well in a world of unlimited possibilities is
harder still, perhaps too hard."
~Barry Schultz - *The Paradox of Choice*

We will make decisions with enduring ramifications in our twenties and thirties. Most of these decisions will be made between two (or more) good options. According to Martin & Smyer, The *Meanwhile* feels full and intense because many Millennials recognize the ramifications and the weight of the decisions they are making. Others do not, and consequently take decisions too lightly.

John is now happily married. Over the years, I've been asked why it didn't work out between us. It's a hard question to answer. The simple response is this—he was my best friend but I wasn't "in love" with him. We had the deepest of soul connections but I didn't have mutual feelings. I spent five years wondering if I should marry him. I feared; if I didn't choose him, there wouldn't be another man as faithful and kind.

Even indecision is a decision. There's a reason we're hesitant. John was beyond good to me and good for me. But, I chose to let go of him when the doubt wouldn't go away. It was the hardest decision I have ever made.

I see the fingerprints of God in my life. I look around and see the people in my life and the dreams He is accomplishing and I know God is taking care of me just as He has taken care of John. I work at a church that feels more like a home and I serve with a staff that is nothing short of family.

God has moved in ways I never expected. I got a promotion when there wasn't even a job description. I became the counselor at the church I work at when I didn't even realize that was an option at this point in my career. I had only been there a year and a half. It's a dream job in many ways. I prayed that God would bring me female friends in my same life stage to walk with and He has delivered in the clearest of ways. I have been encircled, encouraged and fought for by these women. Their hearts and truths are the greatest of gifts.

I know God loves me because through John and his family's care, I came to experience God's lavish love firsthand. John and his family were an undeserved gift. Despite the difficulty of letting him go, God introduced me to the version of Himself John and his family knew.

In our lives, we will say goodbye to important people, places and provisions. Over the years, I have missed my friend even though I felt like I had to let him go. You can still grieve and have peace about a decision. To truly let go and move forward takes time. Sometimes, it takes a long time. But we move forward by entrenching ourselves in what God is doing now.

We need to deal with the emotions surrounding the loss but we also need to shift our focus. We need to focus on the "what is" instead of the "what if." We talk to God over and over and then eventually, the weight of it is over. If you need to say goodbye to someone or something important, complete the Goodbye Letter exercise at the end of this chapter.

I had a decision to make when I left Colorado. Would I stay in seminary or would I return home? It felt like life or death. Taking decisions seriously means we acknowledge our decisions have consequences (positively or negatively). That's a key to adulthood.

Jerry Sittser says, "We believe there is only one way out. All the other ways are dead ends, every one of them a bad choice. Meanwhile, a nagging question hovers in the back of our minds. What if we make the wrong decision?" It's too simple to say that if we line up our choices just right, things will work out the way we hope. If we choose this church, will we miss out on the community God destined for us? If we say no to this one dinner invitation, will we be invited again? Most decisions are not life and death decisions. Think about the reality of the decision we are making. Are they always as huge as we fear?

When I felt anxiety about whether or not to stay in Colorado, God's voice led me back to the mountains. I made a decision (out of fear) to change my degree program but even then, God guided me to a better decision. In His grace and provision, He opened the right doors and I found a place back where I started. Freewill delayed the journey but God used that time to change me. God works all things out for His Kingdom purposes (Romans 8:28).

We make our plans but God determines our steps. His goodness and his sovereignty is the canopy to every choice we make.

We have the freedom to call an audible because of God's provision and grace. My indecision about seminary prolonged my graduation by a year. At the time, it felt like failure or punishment. But, in hindsight, that time was a gift. We never know what God will do after we say "no" to the good thing. God used that extra year of Colorado to do better things.

If I had graduated when I originally planned to, I would have missed out on making some of the best friends and memories I have from Colorado. I might have never found my passion for counseling again. Or learned how to be responsible *to* people, not *for* them.

We get so caught up in making the best decision that we waste a lot of time and energy. We fear that if we don't get it right, God will not provide. But, God is already on the other side of every choice we make. There are consequences to our decisions (for better or worse,) but there is always more grace.

My friend Kaitlyn is a truth-teller. She is fierce in loyalty and she is fierce in her pursuit of the Lord. I trust her heart for God and I trust her heart for me. I know that she will speak the truth in love, which is why I often seek her wisdom and advice when making a big decision.

As Kaitlyn instructs, "When making a decision, see where God is moving and go there." The Holy Spirit will lead us where we ought to go.

Here's the bottom line: we have the power to choose but God will guide us (if we let Him). Think of the Israelites. God was leading them to the Promised Land when they cowered in fear instead. Their disobedience led to death and forty years of wandering.

John 14:16-17 says, "And I will ask the Father, and he will give you another advocate to help you and be with you forever—the Spirit of truth." God has given the Holy Spirit, the Wonderful Counselor, to guide us along the way. If you are unsure of what to do, ask Him. He'll show you. As you plead for direction, read His Word and ask Him to speak to you. Open your eyes and your ears to what He might be revealing. We just need to be brave and trust the nudge the Spirit is giving. Proverbs 1:33 says, "whoever listens to me will dwell secure and will be at ease." If He seems quiet, keep listening.

I may be speaking out of turn but if you are anything like me, you may be scared to make major decisions. And that's okay. It is scary to choose when you don't know where the choice will leave you. I was unprepared for the desperation and loneliness that came after I broke up with John. In her wisdom, Kaitlyn told me, "If you were the one who chose to let him go, you can't be the victim and the persecutor at once." Those words cut deep, but she was right. We have to own the choices we make. That's part of growing up.

Whatever your choice, consider these steps:

1. **What possible options and/or directions do you have? Be specific and pray as you write.**

   Make a pro/con list or a flow-chart of your options.

2. **Continue reading God's Word and pray about the decision and all of the possible options. Write down what you hear God say.**

   As you read, is there a certain message God is giving you? As you pray, are you experiencing a pause, nudge or doubt? In my experience, God uses a pause to tell me to wait. It is not yet time to move as there is more to evaluate. When I feel a nudge, God is telling me to go. And, when I experience doubt, I don't (for now). How about you? Is God speaking to you? Do you hear His voice leading or are you feeling a gut check or doubt?

3. Seek wise counsel. Take notes.

Find people (like Kaitlyn) who are pursuing the Lord. I am thankful for the relationship I have with my parents because I frequently lean on their counsel and wisdom. Who in your life can you ask for guidance from?

4. Research.

As I worked through my decision to leave or continue seminary, I interviewed a woman who had a counseling degree but hadn't chosen to practice. She decided to work as a college advisor and found it immensely fruitful. When you find yourself in an indecisive place, seek out the knowledge found in people who have made a similar decision, in books, and in articles.

5. Evaluate.

Between your research, assessment and conversations, what is God revealing?

6. Be aware.

Is God using a sign or third-party conversation to help in your decision-making? Be certain to heed it even if you don't initially like what it says.

7. Compare notes. Is there a decision rising to the top?

8. Talk again with people you trust. Let them know your latest thinking and heed what they say.

9. Make a decision. Choose and act.

You're probably still scared. I get it. But, we can get stuck in decision-making. That itself is a decision.

9. Re-Evaluate.

Here's the best part. We have the freedom to re-evaluate many of our decisions. After a month of living out the choice you've made, re-assess and see if God has confirmed the decision and if there is peace. If there is unease or angst, re-evaluate. Is God showing you a different direction to take?

"I, wisdom, dwell together with prudence; I possess knowledge and discretion." (Proverbs 8:12, NIV). That word wisdom means listening to advice and accepting instruction. The use of prudence here means keeping quiet and giving thought to his or her steps. We need both to decide.

When making a decision, ask yourself—"Is it right? Is it admirable? Is it lovely, praise-worthy and noble?" (Philippians 4:8). Think back to your values and the man or woman you are becoming. It's easier to commit and say "yes" or "no" to things if we know who we want to be. I truly believe God will show us the way. We just need to give thought to our ways. Pursue selflessness, righteousness and love in whatever decision you are making. God will bless your obedience. The Lord granted me healing only after I made tough choices and obeyed.

QUESTIONS FOR THE MEANWHILE:

1. What is one tough decision you are pleased with the way you made it? What is one you might do differently?

2. What decisions are ahead? Walk through the steps above to help you make the decision.

3. How is fear stopping you from making this decision, or making the decision you believe is right?

4. In what ways are you currently catastrophizing (believing or fearing the worse)?

Scripture to Memorize:

"Have I not commanded you? Be strong and courageous. Do not be afraid; do not be discouraged, for the Lord your God will be with you wherever you go." (Joshua 1:9, NIV).

Counselor's Corner

Write a Goodbye Letter

At times, we may be stuck in decision-making because we haven't let go of someone or something from our past. Many find it helpful to write a **no-send** (emphasis on the not sending part) letter to these important people, places or experiences of their past. Every letter should include:

1. Date
2. Salutation
3. Body
   a. What are you holding onto?
   b. What do you miss about that person or place?
   c. What will you always remember?
   d. Why were they important to you?
   e. What are you grateful for?
   f. Why do you need to move on?
   g. What is one hope for that person or place?
   h. What will you look forward to instead of holding on?
9. Say Goodbye
10. Complimentary Close (e.g. Sincerely, Thank You, Best)

Sample:

Date

Dear [Blank],

I have been thinking about you a lot lately. I keep thinking about [blank] and how you and I would [blank]. I miss the way you [blank] and I miss how I felt [blank] around you. I want you to know that [blank] and I hope you know what you meant to me. I am writing this goodbye letter because [blank]. There are a few specific things I want to tell you: [blank]. I need to let you go because [blank]. I may miss you moving forward but instead of focusing on you and I, I am going to focus on [blank]. Thank you for [blank]. I hope [blank] for you.

Sincerely,
[Blank]

PART FOUR
ROOTED

"But there I have another name. You must learn to know me by that name. This was the very reason why you were brought to Narnia, that by knowing me here for a little, you may know me better there."
~C.S. Lewis's character Aslan -
The Chronicles of Narnia

Chapter Eighteen
#Adulting

"I drink coffee because adulting is hard.
Without it, I'm basically a 2 year old
whose blankie is in the washer."
~Sweatpants and Coffee

I went on a mission trip with 80 high school students. One of my responsibilities was driving the ten-passenger van across the entire state of Texas. It was scary enough until I told my mom about the trip. "Are any adults going with you guys?" Why yes, mom. I'm going.

My generation has coined a lot of terms. One of these is "adulting." It's hard to miss the irony. I found a lot of funny things when I looked up the definition of adulting:

- "Adulting means to do grown up things and hold responsibilities such as a 9-5 job, a mortgage/rent, a car payment, or anything else that makes one think of grown-ups."

- "A desire to hide beneath a homemade bed-sheet fort to color with crayons or the desire to run away."

It's funny but it's also true. I've never wanted to run away more than I do as an adult. Why? Because adulting is hard. In the first few months of work, I was able to save a few thousand dollars thanks to living at home. I felt so proud of myself, so adult, until the real world played a joke on me. Between the shocks going out on my car and a mislabeled emergency room I mistook for an urgent care, I was out $4,000. Welcome to the real world.

According to Jeffrey Arnett, there are three criteria for becoming an adult. First, one must accept responsibility for one's self. Second, one must make independent decisions. And lastly, one must become financially independent.

Henry Cloud summarizes this list in *Changes that Heal* by asserting; "becoming an adult is the process of gaining authority over our lives."

An adult is one who takes ownership of one's beliefs, actions and thoughts without relying on the approval of others.

An adult knows who they are and has found an area of real expertise in which they thrive.

I can come across as wishy-washy. I rely so much on other people's approval of me that I filter every decision through several people before ever making a decision. There is wisdom in seeking counsel but we must filter that wisdom. I have become paralyzed from fear that someone will disapprove of me.

In his book, Cloud outlines several skills to become *mature* (emphasis added) adults under the authority of God. Below is a sampling:

- Reevaluate Beliefs

- Disagree with Authority Figures

- See Parents and Authority Figures Realistically

- Make Your Decisions

- Practice Disagreeing

- Recognize and Pursue Talents

- Recognize the Privileges of Adulthood

- Discipline Yourself

- Submit to Others Out of Freedom

- Do Good Works

- Become a "Pharisee Buster"

- Appreciate Mystery and the Unknown

- Love and Appreciate People Who Are Different

◈ ◈ ◈

Communication

I have a hard time using my voice. I always have. When we were kids, Lindsey would have to order my Happy Meal because I was too scared to talk to people. When I was 19, I went through the line at Subway. I watched in horror as the woman behind the counter smothered mayonnaise, all over my sandwich, even though I hadn't asked for it. I said nothing as she just kept squeezing the condiment bottle.

When I walked out of the restaurant, my parents asked what happened and as I explained my dramatic tale, they told me we weren't leaving until I went into Subway and asked for a new sandwich. This was before I knew what a panic attack was. My palms were sweaty, my voice was shaky and I felt like I was having a hot flash. I mustered up the courage to go back into the restaurant and through a quivering voice, asked for a new sandwich. These days, when I have a hard time finding my voice, I think of the mayonnaise story.

A key aspect of adulthood is learning to navigate difficult conversations. Ann Voskamp says we were made to do hard and holy things. I can think of few things more "adult" than learning to speak the truth in love. I remember the first miscommunication I had with a co-worker. And I remember the first time I had to ask that same co-worker for forgiveness.

You'll face discussions about raises and benefits at your place of employment. You'll fight through sticky friendships that feel one-sided but are still worth fighting for. You'll have to learn how to express your needs, pains and wants in relationships. You'll need to courageously see your mistakes and learn to ask for forgiveness.

As a counselor, I coach people on how to communicate. Sometimes I want to say, "Do as I say and not as I do."

One powerful communication tool is to use "I feel" statements when having a difficult conversation. An "I feel" statement looks like this: I *feel* hurt *when* I'm uninvited to Thursday night dinners *because* I feel left out. Every "I feel" statement involves three parts: feel, when and because. By using a personal pronoun and focusing on the feelings surrounding an interchange or situation, it takes the blame off the hearer of your conversation and provokes dialogue instead of defense.

A key piece of decision-making, disagreeing or having a hard conversation is finding our voice. We have to find the skills and the courage to ask for a new sandwich when we're handed one covered in mayonnaise.

Money

On the first night of college, my friends and I waved goodbye to our parents and looked at each other, wondering what we were supposed to do now. We were on our own, weren't we? There were no curfews or parents taking responsibility. With sheer glee, we piled into cars and did as any sensible college freshman would do; we went and ate our weight in pizza and ice cream.

As an adult, we have total freedom to make our decisions. We get to choose how we spend our time, what we do with our money and whom we do life with. The first large dollar purchase I splurged on was a baby pink designer purse I bought for a Christmas party. Not only did I buy the purse but I bought the silver shoes, pink sequined dress and jewelry to go with it. Now that's a privilege.

With privilege comes responsibility. Buying that purse, shoes, dress and jewelry meant I didn't have as much for gas money. We may have the freedom but we also have a duty—to act like adults. If we have the freedom to spend, we have the responsibility to cover our expenses and the responsibility to give.

My salary used to fluctuate based on the number of clients I would see. While there were some months I felt like I was feasting, there were others that felt like a famine. I had to save for the leaner times.

I wanted to give regularly to my church too. Only after college did I learn the truth of Matthew 6:21. "For where your treasure is, there your heart will be also." No wonder money is such a personal topic. We need it to live, to survive. There are those drowning in credit card debt, trying to pay student loans, or struggling to provide. It is not healthy to be greedy but it is terrifying to watch a bank account dwindle and to wonder, *how will we make ends meet?*

Certain money decisions make it hard to see the light whether in debt, spending or even gambling. It reminds me a little of Alice and Wonderland. We get bored or scared and the next thing we know, we're following a white rabbit down the rabbit hole. If you need help with budgeting or paying off debt or loans, seek advice from someone who manages money well. This person may have the title "financial planner" or they may simply have effective financial habits.

Take the money class called Financial Peace University. Through discipline, we can find peace amidst the anxiety and stress of budget needs and financial issues. To find a class near you, visit: https://www.daveramsey.com/fpu/classes. A wise man once said, travel light in your twenties and thirties. Are we traveling light or are we gathering all kinds of baggage and debt?

Commitment

Our generation lacks responsibility in two specific areas: commitment and timeliness. We wait until the last minute to commit for fear something better will come along. We are flaky and change plans when we realize we'd rather be somewhere else, with someone else, doing something else. We show up late because in our minds, we're busier than you and we value our time more than yours.

Every time we are late or non-committal, we are choosing. We think we are stalling but in reality we are making a decision and communicating a message about worth to others. So who's more valuable? Us or them? I understand we live in an over-committed society but I also believe God said let our "yes" be a "yes" and our "no" be a "no" (Matthew 5:37). Let's focus on margin and value so that we can commit more freely.

An important piece to committing is scheduling. Whether out of insecurity or fear of being alone, I pack people into my schedule. I don't want to lose touch with friends and I don't want to miss out on something fun so I fill up my calendar. I plan dinners a month in advance and say, "yes" to just about every social invitation. And guess what happens? I am so exhausted by the time that dinner rolls around a month later, I end up having to cancel. Be sure to allow for the spontaneous. Create margins in your schedule so that you are rested enough to love and give freely.

Make Your Own Decisions

Henry Cloud describes a "Pharisee buster" as one who sheds the legalism that can creep into our faith. We must let go of all the ways we are trying to earn approval because this eats away at our soul.

Cloud lists barriers to adulthood. A few of these include; a fear of disapproval, guilt, need for permission, fear of failure, and distorted thinking and dependency.

It's exhausting to be consumed with what everyone else thinks. It doubles or triples our decision-making time. I personally lost confidence in my God-given wisdom because of my dependence on others' approval.

Cloud says, "You have only one God. Listen to Him." Full-blown adults are capable to listen and respond. Trust yourself. As you listen to God's voice you know what to do and what not to do.

Adulting is hard. **Growing up takes time as does learning what all that health insurance jargon means.** Have you ever heard the old adage "fake it until you make it?" I think that's what it means to be an adult. Be a big girl and work that 9 to 5 job, but if you're in bed by 8pm or coloring with crayons, that's ok. Don't be so much of an adult that you forget to laugh at yourself or have some fun. We're all just learning. I'm pretty sure that's why it's a verb—we're *growing* up. We're *adulting*.

QUESTIONS FOR THE MEANWHILE:

1. What area(s) of your life do you find more difficult to "adult" in? How can you grow in these areas?

2. In what ways can you exercise freedom with responsibility?

3. What is one hard and holy thing you must do this week? What is the first step in following through with it?

4. What can you change on your calendar to better say "yes" or "no"?

5. Where can you add more margin in your life?

Chapter Nineteen
Friendship

"There are some things you can't share without
ending up liking each other and knocking
out a twelve-foot mountain troll is one of them."
~J.K. Rowling -
Harry Potter and the Sorcerer's Stone

Aspen trees are the most beautiful trees I have ever seen. In Colorado, I spent hours sitting on my balcony watching their leaves glitter in the sunlight and savoring the richness of their colors every fall. I would drive into the mountains, ablaze in the reds, oranges and yellows. These treasured trees taught me many lessons over the years. My favorite? All Aspen trees share a root system. If you uproot one Aspen, you have to uproot them all.

I thought I could do life alone. Post-college, I assumed I had it all figured out and that I didn't need companions. But, the reality is God created us to live in community. Creation was not made perfect until Eve was given to Adam. We all need to be deeply connected with others. We all need community.

Do you remember the Girl Scouting song: "Make new friends but keep the old. One is silver, the other gold?" The friendships you had in high school and college may change over the years. But, in holding onto those, don't crowd out your new life. Expect to create new memories, and expect to meet new friends. When I moved to Colorado, I made the mistake of covering every blank space on my apartment walls and filling every picture frame with pictures of my friends and family back home. I didn't leave any room for the people I would meet in this new phase of life. When I had a new photo from one of our mountain adventures, I didn't have any space to hang it up.

Growing up, I remember wearing matching friendship bracelets. Back then, you thought you'd be friends forever. The reality is very few friendships are lifelong and most are seasonal.

Bill Hybels suggests that to simplify and prioritize our relationships, we have to become aware of our 72, 12 and 3. Jesus had three spheres of relationships, including 72 acquaintances, 12 disciples and two sets of three who were his innermost circles.

Become aware of who is in your root system. At the end of this chapter is an exercise to help you do this. Tend to lifelong friendships as well as make room for new ones. Cultivate friends in your life stage as well as friends who might be in an entirely different season. Spend time with friends who are older and younger than you. Re-evaluate your friendships. Invest your time where time is being given, recognizing that in certain seasons, some will have more or less to give which is completely okay.

Friendships are meant to ebb and flow. Be a loyal friend and love people well, but realize it's important for friendships to be healthy, two-way relationships.

There's no need to be dramatic and cut someone out of your life. But do discern who to invest more time with and who to potentially let go of. Take some relational risks. In college, it is easier to meet people in the classroom or in a student organization. How are we supposed to meet someone while we work in isolation in our cubicle? Sign up for that small group or join an intramural team. Volunteer to bring the donuts to Sunday School class or invite an acquaintance to coffee. If we want friends and we crave intimacy, we need to take the risk to meet someone new and we need to make room for them in our lives.

My Spheres

I took a relational risk when I moved back to Houston and joined my small group. It was one of the best decisions I've ever made. Kelly and I first met in our small group. She's four years younger and my reminder that it's important to have people in our spheres ahead and behind us in years.

Kelly is a champion of a friend. Really. I have known few others as good at celebrating as she. She's one of the biggest cheerleaders I have ever known. You can find her calling her friends weekly to check-in and see how they are doing. You can find her lost in a book because of the desire to learn and grow. Or, you can find her toasting a best friend at a shower, loving a friend on her birthday, and dropping off a meal to a friend needing a hug (me included). Kelly has this special gift of making you feel like a million bucks. I know all of her other friends feel it too.

I have felt God patch up past wounds, old doubts and current fears from spending time with Kelly. There are hard parts to Kelly's story. Really hard. She has walked through things I never will and yet she still chooses to believe in the goodness and provision of our Father, the Fulfiller of desire. She reminds me how thirsty we can be at this age and when I watch her choose Jesus and celebrate, I am encouraged to do the same. Want to hear a part of her story? Be sure to read the foreword she wrote at the beginning of this book.

I also have a friend named Jamie who is six years older than me. With that age gap comes more life experience, more pruning and as I've learned, greater humility. She and I met after a mutual friend said we were similar people. What an honor to be compared to her.

Jamie's mom died when Jamie was 29. Jamie didn't cower or hide; she continued to seek the Father. Jamie has had to be strong for her family and be the nurturer for her dad and two brothers. And she's had to keep living and making decisions in the midst of her grief.

I yearn for Jamie's input and advice. As a woman a few years ahead of me, I need her perspective on things.

I have been given the gift of good friends over the years. 2am friends is what I like to call them. Friends I can call anytime, day or night, and they'll be there. These are the people who see your ugly side and like you anyway. One of my longest-standing friendships is with my dear friend, a sister really—named Alissa. We met in the fourth grade and actually did have matching friendship necklaces. We laugh because we are really different people. Honestly, that's probably why we are such good friends. We see each other's blind spots, and we balance one another out.

Despite our differences, Alissa and I have similar hearts. We both love people and believe in the power of kindness towards others. I love her more than anything.

Over the years, Alissa has been my greatest teammate. We were even nicknamed the "Dynamic Duo" in high school. Our junior year, she sat cross-legged on my bedroom floor for hours, helping me fold my laundry so I could finish packing in time to leave for work at a summer camp. She has always been there.

I was Alissa's maid of honor on her wedding day. She and her husband got married on a deliriously beautiful beach in Jamaica. "Somewhere Over the Rainbow" played as she walked down the aisle, and I wept like a baby. I couldn't have been happier for my best friend. She was marrying the best kind of man. That's the beauty of a lifelong friend. You get the privilege of sharing every season with them.

Family Ties

"The family that [blanks] together, stays together." That was our family's mantra growing up, and it still seems to reign supreme. When we are home for Christmas, this might mean going on a family walk or cooking dinner together. Growing up, this meant going on a family vacation or going to see a movie at the local theatre. Family is an innate part of our root system.

I realize how sweet (and rare) of a gift it is to genuinely like my family, to have parents who show love to one another, and to have a family who loves Jesus and loves me. I know this is not everyone's story and that makes my heart break.

Sharing a root system with your family may have hurt you. It may still be hurting you. And for that, I am so deeply sorry. I know there are some of you who might wish you were part of a different root system. Based on the stories I've heard from friends and from clients,

I can't blame you. But, what I can promise you is that we have the unconditional love of a Father who will never stop wanting you or me. The pain and longing that comes from the wound of a family is one of the deepest kinds. After all, you not only share a name but you share heritage, heartstrings and DNA.

My time in Denver tested my relationships within my family. I changed the roles up the minute I got messy. But, my family stuck with me. I needed their prayers, their wisdom and their guidance. They were there every step of the way.

My sister Lindsey is another essential part of my root system. Lindsey has a zest for life that I often lack. She is quick to pose for a picture, take an adventure or let go of something painful. I need Lindsey in my root system to remind me to live life fully.

Root systems are essential to being a twenty and thirty-something. We need our families and friends to be tied to us in the deepest kind of way. I know that if I were uprooted again, I would have several trees transplanted along with me. Root systems teach us, challenge us and support us. To be rooted is to be in relationship with God, with self and with others. Thanks to them, you're never going to be alone.

QUESTIONS FOR THE MEANWHILE:

1. Who are your friends behind or ahead of you in age? Who are your friends in the same season of life as you? And who are your lifelong friends? Who are you a friend to, in each of these ways? Take the time to write them a thank-you note for being rooted with you.

2. Evaluate the friends in your circle. Who are your 72? Your 12? Your 3? Who is on the outside you would like to bring into a sphere and whom might you need to spend more or less time with?

3. How would you describe your relationship with your family? What is your role in healing certain wounds? In solidifying what God wants cultivated?

4. In what ways can you meet the needs of your family and friends this week?

5. What relational risks do you need to take?

Counselor's Corner

Chart your Friendships

Use the diagram below to fill in your two sets of three, your set of 12 and your set of 72.

Navigating Healthy Relationships

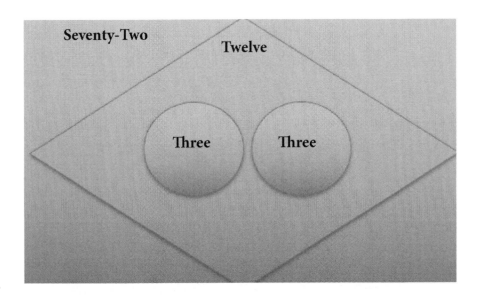

I want to tread lightly, as I don't know the rejection, pain or abuse you may have experienced in your family or in other relationships, either growing up or currently. But, I think it is healthy and wise to begin looking at these severed ties and wounds as a twenty or thirty-something before we have families of our own. If you're reading this and it resembles any part of your story, it might be a good time to seek out a pastor, Christian counselor or mentor to begin talking about your family and the wounds you may carry with you. We need the people who are placed in our root system and they need us too. Ask God to show you the role He wants you to play in your family and friendships alike.

We were rooted in family before we were rooted in any other relationship, which means we learned how to grow and what shape to take from those family members we were planted with. As a Millennial, it is good to be an individual and begin to separate from our parents. It is also good to love and honor those family members, no matter the wounds or boundaries that might be in place.

Chapter Twenty
A $3.00 Shot of Espresso

"I want a life that sizzles and pops and makes me laugh
out loud. And I don't want to get to the end, or to
tomorrow, even, and realize that my life is a collection
of meetings and pop cans and errands and receipts
and dirty dishes. I want to eat cold tangerines and sing
out loud in the car with the windows open and wear
pink shoes and stay up all night laughing and paint
my walls the exact color of the sky right now. I want to
sleep hard on clean white sheets and throw parties and
eat ripe tomatoes and read books so good they make
me jump up and down, and I want my
everyday to make God belly laugh, glad that
he gave life to someone who loves the gift."
~Shauna Niequist - *Cold Tangerines*

By my twenty-fifth birthday, winter had finally lifted. I no longer
sought control. God was rightly placed on His throne. My birthday is in October, when the first cold snap of the year comes to Colorado. My beloved Aspen leaves turn yellow, orange and red.

I was planning a day trip to Aspen with Rachel and Erin, and I
had been looking forward to it for weeks. It's a five-hour drive from
Denver to Aspen, and the three of us loaded into my car and began
our journey. It was the dreamiest day. I was in the driver's seat flying

free, grateful for my life and who I was becoming. The sun melted my icy bones as I looked at a bluebird sky and purple mountain majesties.

None of us talked for fear of breaking the holy hush. My soul met body along that five-hour drive. It was no longer in transit across the thousand miles from Houston to Denver. I felt grateful for the journey the Lord had taken me on as we drove along the winding road and over bumbling springs.

In Aspen the colors were beaming. They were like high-flying flags in the wind. We got out and I spent $3.00 on the tiniest cup of espresso I had ever seen. Instead of complaint, I felt glee. I laughed as I paid the cashier. The three of us walked to the edge of town where free gondola rides were being offered to the top of the mountain. *Another gift*, I thought. *These rides usually cost an arm and a leg.* I asked Erin to take my picture in front of the mountains. I lifted my arms up high and opened them out wide. With a smile on my face, I thought, *I am home.*

It was good to be alive.

Bob Goff says, "I want my life to be full of abandon, whimsy and love." Me too, Bob. Me too. The *Meanwhile* can be hard enough on its' own. We don't need to add our misery.

When was the last time we loved someone more than ourselves? When was the last time we smiled at a stranger? Let someone cut us in line at the grocery store?

Life is best lived undone.

I love that word. Whimsy. It means fanciful, lovely and unique. I read that description and I remember our Aspen trip fondly.

We all need more whimsy. We need to let loose and have some fun. We need to create, travel, and experience something new. I want to give a champagne toast, learn how to bake bread, make a killer charcuterie plate, throw clay on a potter's wheel, sleep-in, walk a beach barefoot, and pop some confetti. The list goes on.

My small group and I each made a bucket list of all the things we want to see, try and do. Kelly bought a new camera and is taking photography lessons. Amy is attending painting class. Kinzi is taking karate. I went to Vegas to see Celine Dion with girlfriends. Part of enjoying our twenties and thirties is exploring. Try something new this month. Decide to do one fun thing each week. Take a class at your local community college or learn how to bake a cake and decorate cookies.

I have several bucket lists. I have one for this season of life and I have one for my lifetime as well. The list I have for this season includes items I want to do as a single woman. The lifetime list has items I'd like to experience in a different season. Some of the items are already crossed off:

1. ~~Write a book~~
2. ~~Take a trip to Los Angeles to visit my sister~~
3. ~~Give back financially~~
4. ~~Lead a small group~~
5. Purchase my home
6. ~~Buy and care for a dog~~
7. Take a road trip to Fredericksburg, Texas
8. Volunteer two times/month
9. Live on my own in an apartment or home

I'm an advocate for seeing the world, trying something new and making a bucket list. But, let's not allow exploration to become self-absorption. It's all about moderation. If we can spend money on trips, we should be tithing as well. If we find time to go out on a Thursday evening, we can find time to give back. I have learned a lot from Ann Voskamp. I was challenged when she said: "empty, poured-out buckets are actually the fullest buckets." It is a good thing to pursue whimsy. But, it is a holy thing to pursue love and abandon. Sometimes, they are one in the same.

At the end of the day, Erin, Rachel and I decided to snap some pictures of the Aspen trees before heading back to Denver. We parked at the base of the mountain and jumped over a ditch to walk through a field of trees. They were so bright. It looked like a star had burst over night and sprinkled its remains down here on earth. The sunlight hit the yellow leaves, and as I watched the leaves twinkle and shake, I could feel the warmth of the sunbeam.

When we were done with our photo-shoot, we headed back to the car. Erin went ahead of Rachel and me in order to help us across the ditch. When it was my turn, I jumped to make the leap, but before my feet hit the ground, I felt my back hit the cold, wet ground. My feet had slipped underneath me and I wiped out right there in the mud. It looked like I was making a snow angel in the muck of fall. My plaid button-down was stuck to the mud and my black leggings had leaves pinned to the outside of them. Erin and Rachel gasped. I couldn't stop laughing as tears began to roll down my cheeks. I hadn't laughed like that in years, and as I bellowed, I felt like I had finally caught up on lost time. I was happy.

As we made our way back through the mountains, passing the Aspen trees and crossing springs, I felt something I hadn't felt since moving to Denver. I smiled. It was contentment. I no longer wanted something else. I wanted this, right here. I wanted to be a single woman figuring this life thing out with two of her best friends. And there was nothing I would have changed about that day. It was a day full of whimsy, fun and love. I want to make every day that sweet.

QUESTIONS FOR THE MEANWHILE:

1. Describe a time in your life when you felt grateful for the moment and place you were in.

2. How have you helped to create peace and contentment in the lives of people you encounter every day?

3. In what ways can gratefulness uproot envy? Loneliness? Complaining?

4. What are you thankful for right now? (Think about where you live, the people in your life, your employment status, an opportunity the Lord has given you, provision, etc.)

Counselor's Corner

Make a Playlist

Listening to music can bring great hope, comfort and whimsy. Take the time to create your playlist. Include songs that bring back good memories, have lyrics of truth and make you want to sing along. Below are some of the songs we listened to on our way to Aspen and others I listened to as I wrote this book:

1. "Ever Be" by Bethel

2. "Let it Go" by James Bay

3. "The One You Need" by Shane & Shane

4. "After the Storm" by Mumford and Sons

5. "Windows are Rolled Down" by Amos Lee

6. "Turn Down the Music" by Shane & Shane

7. "Another Man's Shoes" by Drew Holcomb & the Neighbors

8. "Below my Feet" by Mumford and Sons

9. "Trust in You" by Lauren Daigle

10. "Come Alive (Dry Bones)" by Lauren Daigle

11. "First" by Lauren Daigle

12. "Good Good Father" by Chris Tomlin

13. "It is Well" by Bethel

14. "Psalm 23" by Shane & Shane

15. "Keep Breathing" by Ingrid Michaelson

16. "Timshel" by Mumford and Sons

17. "Before the Throne" by Shane & Shane

18. "Love is Waiting" by Brooke Fraser

19. "Beautiful, Scandalous Night" by Robbie Seay Band

Chapter Twenty-One
Freedom

"That tree whose leaves are trembling: it is yearning for
something. That tree so lovely to see acts as if it wants
to flower: it is yearning for something."[2]
~Diego Hurtado de Mendoza - *Stanza*

"Therefore, there is now no condemnation for those who are in
Christ Jesus," the professor said as he threw a heavy set of chains
to the ground (Romans 8:1). The room was silent. I looked at the
chains on the floor and then back up at the professor. *Was it like this
every week?* I thought. The chains stayed on the floor for the remainder
of class that day. I took two classes from Dr. Moore. My final semester
was also spent with him as my group supervisor for my two off-site
counseling internships. On the first day of class each year, Dr. Moore
began by throwing those chains to the ground. We were free, and he
wanted us to experience liberty.

Freedom was something I had never really known prior to moving
to Denver. My practically perfect ways and my queen tendencies had
never allowed it. But then in the mess and fragility I learned that light
shines through broken glass.

While doing a project for my Biblical Interpretation course, I
did a word study on First Peter 2:16. "Live as free people, but do not
use your freedom as a cover-up for evil; live as God's slaves" (NIV).

I learned the Greek word for slaves is *doulos*, not a title of shame but of honor. The slavery it describes is one of self-realization. It is the awareness and acceptance of the slave's need for and dependence on God.

God does not impose His will on His *doulos*. The slave has not experienced a forced loss of freedom but rather the slave has chosen a position of obedience to the God he or she serves.

After completing my project, I went by Dr. Moore's office to ask if I could borrow his chains. I wanted to be able to show my class what freedom in binding oneself in service looked like. Dr. Moore wasn't in his office, so I left him a note proposing my idea. The next day I got an email from Dr. Moore telling me to come by his office to pick up the chains.

When I arrived at his office I saw a gift bag tied with a white bow. "This is for you," he said. As I opened up the bag and looked beneath the tissue paper, I saw a pair of chains just like his. Below the chains was also a tiny jar of healing balm. I didn't know what to say.

I asked, "Are you sure I can have these?"

He looked at me, with serious eyes, "Of course. These are my gift to you. After all, you're free aren't you? And don't you believe that you have the gift of healing too?"

A few months later, I woke up early one morning in order to get a start on my day. I realized something. I felt lighter, like ten pounds lighter. The chains I had been wearing around my neck had fallen off. The wrestling was over. I had cast the burden before the Lord's feet. I had finally given up playing God, and the true God was rightly on His throne. The battle was over. I was free.

Later that night, my roommates were out to dinner. It was dark outside, and I was home alone. I walked into the living room, turned on the lights and lit some candles. I moved our ottoman toward the couch and pushed the side chair against the wall. I walked into the kitchen and picked out a song to play. I shuffled my iPod to one of my favorite worship songs and cranked up the music, loud. I walked back into the middle of the living room, and I began to dance. I sang along to the music as I lifted my hands high and twirled around in circles. I talked to God and spun around and around as I praised Him in a blur of candlelight and peace. I was new. I was free. I was redeemed.

The song ended, and I dropped to my knees. I put my head to the ground and opened my palms to the sky. *Father God, thank you. Thank you for bringing me to the mountains and for speaking to me tenderly. Thank you for giving me a new name and helping me find my roots.* I laid there with knees to the earth and hands and heart wide open. After a few minutes, I stood and picked another song on the iPod. Tonight I was going to dance. I was going to dance free.

QUESTIONS FOR THE MEANWHILE:

1. Describe a time in your life that you felt free. Why did you feel that way? What did you do?

2. What chains do you need to throw to the floor in order to be free? How can you similarly make it easy for those near you to live in freedom?

3. In what ways has God spoken tenderly to you?

4. What is your reaction to being a voluntary slave of God, His *doulos?*

5. How can you thank God today for being the One to break all of your chains?

Chapter Twenty-Two
Graduation Day

"You DID IT. You right there, yeah, you
DID it, and you stuck it out."
~Lindsey Caldwell

I graduated from Denver Seminary almost three years to the day after graduating from Texas A&M. Everything was different though.
I had once walked across the stage in heels of pride but now I walked
across the stage in wedges of humility. I had a new name, a new set
of eyes, and a new heart. I had learned that this post-college, big-girl
world can be hard, but it can also be deep and life-giving. God is not
a stand-off dictator, but God is personal and near. I no longer felt the
need to attack life with clinched fists. I was ready to live with open
hands. I had tried to place so many other plans, accolades and people
onto the throne of my life, but it is God alone who sits on the throne.
And I was walking in joy—the deep settled confidence that God was
in control.

The band played "Come Thou Fount of Every Blessing." My time
in Denver had not been what I expected, but it was everything I needed.
I smiled as I thought of my Savior, the One who had been there all along.
God had walked with me to that graduation day. In His sovereignty,
He had placed the right people and the right experiences along the way
to prune me, to grow me and to change me. I graduated from college as
Amanda, but on the morning of my seminary graduation, I graduated
as Amanda Grace, a woman who was no longer the perfect child, but
one who was full of grace.

My friend Cassie describes the journey like this: "I am in the *Meanwhile*. Uncharted. But now, I remember being here before. The *Meanwhile* found me when I encountered my first love, when I heard the voice of God for the first time, and when I felt the pain of loss and of healing. Despite the fear, I remember something. I remember the sound of God's steady footsteps alongside me, and I am reminded to trust Him again. That's how I know the *Meanwhile* will come again.

I will encounter the *Meanwhile* on the first day of a new job, in the embarking of marriage, on hearing I will be a mother, and on the first day of rest after many years of labor. Each *Meanwhile* will look different, but it will feel the same. I won't recognize it at first, but if I remember the sound of His footsteps, I will remember the way of seeing that allows for God to show me nothing is for naught. The truth will always remain that the more I seek, the more I will be sought. The *Meanwhile* might be a mystery, but it is also a blessing. It is a travelogue of intertwining journeys, all in the presence of God."

After graduation, I made my way home to Houston. It was the easiest decision I ever made. I didn't even pray much about it because my contented spirit so loudly shouted "home." I moved back to the same city I grew up in, though I now live in a new part of town. I started going by my new name, and I spent time with the family and friends I had left behind three years prior. I learned that while so much was the same, much was different. My *Meanwhile* had brought in a new wave of change, and as I waded out into the waters, I realized I was going to have to find a way to live out my new identity in the place I had always known. There are days this is comfortable and there are days where I find myself still adjusting.

I see things differently nowadays. I hear things differently, and I want things I never thought I would want.

The *Meanwhile* changed me in a way I would have never anticipated. When I lived in Denver, I wanted to be back in Houston. Now that I'm here I realize the questions, loneliness, and longings of the *Meanwhile* can't be cured with a geographic move. I will always be in a *Meanwhile* on this side of Heaven.

God is giving me a chance to cash in on the lessons learned from the change I experienced in Denver. God has given me a new city, new friends and a new job to practice all He has taught me. He has brought me to a familiar place so that I may use my new eyes and wear my new identity. This is my do-over.

I now know who I am, I know the shape of my roots, and the kind of tree I want to be. I am full of grace and held in the hands of God, whom I love more than anything. It hasn't been a flawless or pretty transition at times, but one thing is sure. I refuse to turn my back on God again, even during the blues of a Sunday or in the thirst of my desire. If the treasures of this earth will never satisfy, I want the one thing that does. The *Meanwhile* isn't fulfilled by crossing a finish line. The *Meanwhile* is satisfied in death with eternal life. There is so much more to being a twenty or thirty-something than finding ourselves, landing a good job or finding the one to marry. The *Meanwhile* is about finding Him.

In *The Velveteen Rabbit* Margery Williams says, "It doesn't happen all at once … It takes a long time. That's why it doesn't happen often to people who break easily, or have sharp edges, or who have to be carefully kept. Generally, by the time you are Real, most of your hair has been loved off, and your eyes drop out and you get loose in the joints and very shabby. But these things don't matter at all, because once you are Real you can't be ugly, except to people who don't understand."

The *Meanwhile* is a journey of broken pieces, mended hearts and the truest of beauties. We have to bend so we don't break. We have to deliberately reach out to care and meet needs. We have to be ok being alone (even in relationship) and we have to be ok with ourselves. To be ok with ourselves, we first have to like ourselves. And to like ourselves, we have to get to know ourselves.

This is a journey between you and God. My sister Lindsey explains it like this: "Ambition will eventually get us 'there,' accompanied by God's plan, direction, and faithfulness. But, the reality is, the 'there' will never be all that we want. Maybe that's the lesson. There really is never a 'there.' There never will be a time where we feel settled in our 'there,' and that's why we have to trust and have peace in the '*theres*' that God has for us along the way." If we'll always be in this state of *Meanwhile* on this side of heaven, there's no longer any rush to get "there." Put it that way and we can all just settle down and *be* in the place God has us.

So, give yourself a break. It's going to be okay. It takes time to become. We will only be young once, so go ahead: chase hard after

God, hop on a plane, move across the country, choose to commit. The offer to come to life is an open invite. I want a life full of joy and confetti, but I'm not going to get there without surrendering.

The *Meanwhile* is not a plight to fight or an infection to cure. It is an invitation to come to life. Life will be found in the hands of our good and gracious Father. We find the *Meanwhile* at the crossroads of the broken and beautiful places, where humanity meets the face of God and we are no longer the same. Nothing is for naught in the *Meanwhile*. It all counts, the big and the small. Will you accept God's invitation to life-everlasting on this side of Heaven? He is our only hope that there will be a "there."

QUESTIONS FOR THE MEANWHILE

1. Describe what your meanwhile looks and feels like.

2. What kind of "there" and finish line do you envision for yourself?

3. Imagine that you are writing a book of your life. Write your table of contents with each chapter describing a different part of your life. Naming the chapters can help you conceptualize your travelogue so far. For example, I used "Graduation Day," "Perfect Child," and "A $3 Shot of Espresso." Be sure to add at least one chapter reserved for the future. This will be a place to record your hopes for what is to come.

Chapter Twenty-Three
Suddenly

"She had the feeling that somehow, in the very far-off places, perhaps even in far-off ages, there would be a meaning found to all sorrow and an answer too fair and wonderful to be as yet understood."
~Hannah Hurnard - *Hinds' Feet on High Places*

I bet you're wondering how this story ends. I don't know yet. But that's okay. I can see it unfolding but I still wake up asking God to move. The *Meanwhile* is synonymous with the phrase "in-between." The word *Suddenly* is synonymous with the words "swiftly, quickly, unexpectedly." We serve a God over both. The *Meanwhile* and the *Suddenly*. We serve a God who will be present in the waiting but we also serve a God who can move swiftly, quickly, unexpectedly. It's time to believe in the God of both—the waiting and the moving.

I believe that deep calls to deep (Psalm 42:7). I believe deep questioning brings deep trusting, deep pain brings deep healing, and deep surrendering brings the deepest of joys (Psalm 42:7).

I am in this with you. Like knee-deep-in-the-mud in this with you. Our stories are unfinished because God's not done. That's the beautiful part, isn't it? We never know what He's going to do. We never know how He's going to show up: swiftly, quickly, or unexpectedly. Believe He is able.

The *Meanwhile* didn't kill me, though it often felt like it would. The *Meanwhile* shaped me. I'd rather be Amanda Grace than Amanda any day of the week. If I don't make the focus perfection, it means I can give others freedom too. I refuse to get stuck. No matter my season of life, I am going to celebrate and believe that *this* right here, today, is truly God's best for me (even the spilled coffee and sweatpants I'm currently wearing).

I am going to live alongside my longing. There is something to celebrate every day. The mundane Mondays, the made-it-through-the-week Fridays, and all the moments God shows up. I expected to get kitchen items at a shower or to purchase holiday decorations for a home. But, I got tired of waiting. I decided to live and to celebrate *now*, not *then*.

My apartment is filled with decorations and mementos I treasure. It's been compared to a warm hug. If I had gotten stuck waiting, the walls would have remained bare. Instead, they are full. I have boxes stored with Christmas trees, ornaments from my grandmother, bunny ears and the cutest ceramic pumpkins you've ever seen.

The antidote to change is commitment. Commit to building a home wherever God has placed you. Faith is revealed in us every time we commit. It's the opposite of how I behaved in Colorado. If God got it "right" with me, what would I be doing? How would I be behaving? If God got it "right" with you, what would you be doing? How would you be behaving? Well, since God got it right with me, I am going to plant roots. And every time I decorate my apartment with decorations for the season, I am reminded—God is the God of this season too.

In the years since Colorado, I have practiced what I preach in this story. I've made new friends, but kept the old. I have wept and celebrated with others. I have traveled, made mistakes, learned and grown. I moved to a new city and decided to write a story about change alongside of my leavings. I thought it'd only take a year or two to complete but I should've known better when writing a story about waiting. It took three years and a publication delay to complete. I have learned how to serve and am working to kill the selfishness that resides. I have fumbled and believed, got it right and also had to ask for forgiveness. I have done it all. And at the end, this is what I believe: God is good, all the time. All the time, God is good. No matter how dreary or haphazard your journey seems. Believe. I promise you He is working it all out as we speak. Let's grow deep and wide in the Love and

Truth of God (Colossians 2:7). That's what it means to become rooted in life's limbo. That's what we're supposed to do in the *Meanwhile.*

From one sapling to another,
Amanda Grace

BOOK LIST

As I have navigated the *Meanwhile*, I've learned the importance of reading and the stillness, wisdom, and growth reading brings. Here are a few of my favorites (in alphabetical order):

1. *Anything: The Prayer that Unlocked My God and My Soul* by Jennie Allen

2. The *Bible*

3. *Bittersweet: Thoughts on Change, Grace and Learning the Hard Way* by Shauna Niequist

4. *Changes That Heal: The Four Shifts that Make Everything Better...and That Anyone Can Do* by Henry Cloud

5. *Circle Maker: Praying Circles Around your Biggest Dreams and Greatest Fears* by Mark Batterson

6. *Cold Tangerines: Celebrating the Extraordinary Nature of Everyday Life* by Shauna Niequist

7. *Hinds' Feet on High Places* by H. Hurnard

8. *How to Get a Date Worth Keeping: Be Dating in Six Months or Your Money Back* by Henry Cloud

9. *Meaning of Marriage: Facing the Complexities of Commitment with the Wisdom of God* by T. Keller and K. Keller

10. *One Thousand Gifts: A Dare to Live Fully Right Where You Are* by Ann Voskamp

11. *Simplify: Ten Practices to Unclutter Your Soul* by Bill Hybels

12. *The Will of God as a Way of Life: How to Make Every Decision with Peace and Confidence* by J. Sittser

APPENDIX A

Begin with this list of passages when you are experiencing one of these feelings.

Then as you read the Bible for yourself, add to the list:

When you feel purposeless, read this:

"Good and upright is the Lord; He guides the humble in what is right and teaches them his way … All His ways are loving and faithful … He will instruct [me] in the way chosen for [me]. My eyes are ever on the Lord…Guard my life and rescue me, let me not be put to shame, for I take refuge in you. May integrity and uprightness protect me, because my hope is in you"(Psalm 25: 8-10; 12; 20-21, NIV).

When you feel sad, read this:

"You know what I long for, Lord; you hear my every sigh" (Psalm 38:9, NIV).

When you feel left out, read this:

"You also were included in Christ when you heard the word of truth, the gospel of your salvation. Having believed, you were marked in Him with a seal, the promised Holy Spirit who is a deposit guaranteeing our inheritance until the redemption of those who are God's possession—to the praise of His glory" (Ephesians 1:13, 14, NIV).

When you feel unsure of who to go to, read this:

"Praise be to the Lord, to God our Savior, who daily bears our burdens" (Psalm 68:19, NIV).

When you feel confused, read this:

"Now I know in part; then I shall know fully, even as I am fully known" (2 Corinthians 13:12, NIV).

When you are missing home, read this:

"The Lord is my shepherd; I shall not be in want. He makes me lie down in green pastures, he leads me beside quiet waters, he restores my soul" (Psalm 23:1-3, NIV).

When tempted to compare yourself with others, read this:

"That means we will not compare ourselves with each other as if one of us were better and another worse. We have far more interesting things to do with our lives. Each one of us is an original" (Galatians 5:26, The Message).

When you fear, read this:

"Be strong. Take courage. Don't be intimidated. Don't give them a second thought because, God your God is striding ahead of you. He's right there with you. He won't let you down. He won't leave you" (Deuteronomy 31:6, The Message).

When you feel lonely, read this:

"According to your love remember me, for you are good … Turn to me and be gracious to me, for I am lonely and afflicted. The troubles of my heart have multiplied; free me from my anguish" (Psalm 25: 7; 16-17, NIV).

"He will give you another Advocate, who will never leave you" (John 14:16, NIV).

When you need help, read this:

"Keep watch over me and keep me out of trouble; Don't let me down when I run to you" (Psalm 25:20, NIV).

"He has taken my hand because I don't know the way, I don't know where I am going. He is my personal guide, directing and shepherding me through rocky and scary country. He is right here to show me what roads to take, making sure I do not fall into the ditch. He is and will do all of these things for me—sticking with me, not leaving me for a second" (Isaiah 42:16, NIV).

"Praise be to the God and Father of our Lord Jesus Christ, the Father of compassion and the God of all comfort, who comforts us in all our troubles, so that we can comfort those in any trouble with the comfort we ourselves receive from God" (1 Corinthians 1:3-4, NIV).

When you feel anxious, read this:

"Cast all your anxiety on him because he cares for you" (1 Peter 5:7, NIV).

Afterword

Brandon Gaide,
Former Associate Pastor of Next Generation Ministries at
Memorial Drive Presbyterian Church

One day a Millennial will be the President of the United States. This is both startling and exciting. Millennials are stereotyped as entitled, self-centered, institution-averse, and even lazy. But we are so much more. In a now-classic article by Tim Urban in The Huffington Post, Urban suggests that Millennials expect their lives to grow not just "greener grass" than that of their parents, but lives that blossom into, "A shiny unicorn on top of the flowery lawn." How will this worldview affect the globe?

We Millennials broadcast our social/professional/personal/culinary lives on every social media outlet we can find. In our desire to be deeply authentic, we share maybe more than we should about ourselves. Our faults are not hard to find. But so are our strengths. Will Millennials be the downfall of Western civilization? Are we a train wreck waiting to come of age?

Of course not.

There's no denying the significant value shifts in our generation. We nod approvingly when we hear David Kinnaman's phrase attempting to give an identity to Millennials: "discontinuously different." In the not-so-distant future, America will change. The church will change. Our social norms will change.

We Millennials are working to change them for the better.

Scholar N.T. Wright said, "Postmodernism is a necessary judgment on the arrogance of modernism." For all the good brought by previous generations, they also brought problems. The "arrogance of modernism" permitted the rise of multiple wars, the rise of the divorce rate, and the fall of interest in religion. Modernism—the confident march of humanity toward a more evolved society—could not deliver on all it promised.

For all the flak Millennials receive, critics often fail to notice what we resolutely believe: we're going to change the world for good. We're too aware of the problems in our world to ignore them. We care too much about our world, our culture, and our "tribes," to miss the opportunity to influence and change our context. Our goal in life goes beyond becoming rooted in the suburbs with 2.5 children and a stable career. Like many who have come before us, we long to make an impact, to leave a mark, to ensure our lives on this earth are well-used.

To that end, Amanda Grace Caldwell enters the picture. Her book is a travelogue, recording her journey from one fascinating stage of maturity to another. In classic Millennial authenticity, she includes the cul-de-sacs and dead-ends along the way, reminding the reader that growth is messy. Amanda Grace's book personifies the cry of a generation, constantly asking, "Do I matter now? Am I significant now?" For Millennials, our point of arrival is not landing a perfect career or dreamy relationship. Instead, it's our lives meaning something to the world.

Amanda Grace sets out to answer how we will know we've "made it," or at least are on the way to our destinations. She dissects her own meaning-making journey, wondering aloud if she's getting closer. My mind goes to a particularly clear example: "When I introduce myself, I'm not sure whether to call myself a woman or a girl." This in-between stage, this meanwhile, is precisely the location where questions of identity and significance become most pressing.

We Millennials are still young, and our worldview is largely untested. We need Amanda Grace's book, and more like it, to courageously and successfully venture into the unknown. We need to struggle with the big questions as we carve our way into positions of leadership and influence. We need faithful people willing to wrestle honestly alongside us with what it means to be a mature, God-honoring adult. How do we come of age in the twenty-first century?

This book is a way point in the maturing of the Millennial generation. Let Amanda Grace's story inspire and accelerate your growth toward faithfulness and significance.

Acknowledgments

My life is filled to the brim with people who have graciously loved and supported me. I believe human connection is one of the greatest gifts God has given us on this side of Heaven. His salvation is the first connection and we build our human connections upon it.

I first want to thank you, Mom and Dad. You have taken care of me from day one and have always pointed me to Jesus. Thank you for being my safe harbor and for making me believe I'm loved, valued, and capable of anything. You two are the greatest gifts in the world. I long to have a family one day so I can carry on your love and legacy. Thank you for teaching me to work hard and for providing the life you did for us as children and now as adults. All that you have done with Caldwell Companies and in the community is nothing short of awe-inspiring. It is a humbling gift to call you mine.

Lindsey, thank you. You are the greatest adventurer I know. I long to be joy-filled like you and every time we talk, you remind me that this life is meant to be enjoyed. Faith is one of your greatest gifts. You make my world so much more fun and full. You daily teach me how to "own it" and enjoy life. I am so proud of the woman you have chosen to become! Thank you for all that you contributed for this story as well. (I recommend you follow my sister Lindsey on ifyoucandreamitdoit. com).

Thank you to my extended family on both sides (in Heaven and here on earth). I am doubly blessed to be linked to such fun, faithful and joy-filled people. Thank you for the gift of calling you "mine" and for the chance to share in the same gene pool and gifts you have cultivated in your lives.

Thank you to my friends. You are precious people to me. Thank you to all who contributed to this story and to those who allowed me to share part of their stories to share my own. Thank you. Thank you for pouring so much life and love into my heart over the years. I really don't know where I would be without each of you. You are all such a gift to me and I know that God will continue to use you in mighty ways to love His people.

Thank you to my church family at Windwood Presbyterian Church where I grew up. There are no words for what our church family meant to me or how it shaped me. Thank you for teaching me about Jesus, what it meant to be the church body, and about love. I miss you all.

Thank you to the Delta Omega Chapter of Kappa Alpha Theta. You helped me become the woman I am today. My favorite college memories come from within the walls of that sorority house and from the friendships I made with some of the best women I know.

Thank you to Mrs. Reily and Mrs. Frank, some of my earliest English teachers. Thank you for instilling in me the love of writing and love for the English language Thank you for believing in me! I love you both and fondly remember sitting in your classrooms.

Thank you to my professors at Texas A&M University for training me to be a student. You cemented the values of what it means to be an Aggie. I was best prepared for the real world by taking classes and meeting with each of you.

Thank you to my professors and the staff at Denver Seminary. What felt like a rollercoaster of three years ended up being the biggest blessing of my life. Thank you for daily teaching us students and pouring into us professionally and personally. The lessons I learned and the challenges I received along the way are who made me into the person I am today.

Thank you to my supervisors in Colorado, the Alternatives and Positive Pathways staff in Denver, and Jill Gilbert here in Houston. Thank you for investing in me as a clinician and as a Daughter of the King.

Thank you to Melonie and the Richards family for being my mentor and my second family in Colorado. You were my lifeblood in a season I was so dry. Thank you for daily and continuing to stand in the gap for me.

Thank you to Britany and the Chambers family (as well as the CCMC staff). Thank you for being like family to me and making work a place I loved to show up to every week. You are precious to me.

Thank you to the TBarM, JH Ranch, and Outback Texas families. It's been an honor to do camp ministry with you.

Thank you to the MDPC staff for welcoming me with open arms when I joined the team. Our church is like home to me and I consider it one of the greatest gifts to serve with each of you. Thank you for the chance to grow professionally, personally and spiritually. I can't imagine being anywhere else.

Thank you to the Bold Vision Publishing staff and especially to Karen who patiently answered my dozens of emails and invested in me personally and professionally. Thank you for caring enough about me to give me the choice to delay. And to my editors, Karen Dockery and Kathryn Porter who made me think and made me a better writer. Thank you!

And ultimately, thank you to God the Creator. Thank you for giving me a love of words and of people. Thank you for the people you dropped in my life along the way. Thank you for wooing us no matter our state or position. Thank you for calling me to be your daughter. It is what makes this life and *Meanwhile* worthwhile.

About the Author

Amanda Grace received her BA in Marketing and a Minor in Creative Writing at Texas A&M University before heading to Littleton, Colorado where she received her Master's in Clinical Mental Health Counseling at Denver Seminary. Amanda Grace served as the President of the Delta Omega Chapter of Kappa Alpha Theta while in college and has spent time serving with the ministries of TBarM and JH Ranch. Amanda Grace has a heart for teenage girls and women of all ages and enjoys the chance to connect with others and hear their stories. She is a member of Houston's First Baptist Church and currently works at Memorial Drive Presbyterian Church as the Counselor-in-Residence and serves in the Relationships Ministry. In her free time, you can find Amanda Grace penning prayers in her journal, checking out a concert or local foodie spot, cooking, taking a yoga class, or going on a long walk or hike. She is a lover of sunflowers, antiques, and chai tea latte's and is most content sitting across the table from a dear friend having a long, good-for-your-soul conversation.

Connect with Amanda Grace at www.agracespace.com

Endnotes

1   Genesis 2:4-3:24.
2   Ibid.
3   Diego Hurtado de Mendoza, *Stanza*. Cambridge University Library, Department of Manuscripts and University Archives, Diego Hurtado de Mendoza: Poems, MS Add.7941